MICROPROCESSORS

MICROPROCESSORS
TECHNOLOGY, ARCHITECTURE, AND APPLICATIONS

DANIEL R. McGLYNN
U.S. Philips Corporation

A Wiley-Interscience Publication

John Wiley & Sons

New York • London • Sydney • Toronto

Library of Congress Cataloging in Publication Data:

McGlynn, Daniel R
  Microprocessors: technology, architecture, and
applications.

  "A Wiley-Interscience publication."
  Bibliography: p.
  Includes index.
  1. Microprocessors. 2. Miniature computers.
I. Title.

TK7888.3.M26   001.6′4   76-137

ISBN 0-471-58414-2

10 9 8 7 6 5 4 3

To My Mother and Father

PREFACE

Recent advances in the field of large-scale-integration semiconductor process technology have made possible substantial reductions in the cost and size of digital logic circuits. In the last decade, computer system building blocks have progressed from discrete components such as single transistors to complex functional integrated circuits containing many logic gates on a single semiconductor "chip." The size and economic advantages of incorporating a large number of arithmetic and logic functions on a single IC chip were of particular interest to manufacturers of pocket calculators and intelligent terminals, and the first proposals for a "computer-on-a-chip" came from such sources.

Although the custom design of a "computer on a chip" had been attempted earlier, the first commercial microprocessors did not appear on the market until 1971. The understanding and market acceptance of any revolutionary new product are slow to come, particularly for a product as complex as a microprocessor. It was several years before the advantages of the versatility of microprocessors were fully comprehended by digital systems designers, and before the manufacturing processes became of sufficient scale for managers to justify the feasibility of new product lines utilizing microprocessors. By 1976, there were over two dozen microprocessors commercially available or announced; they were being produced at the rate of 35,000 per month and were already incorporated in scores of computer terminals, laboratory instruments, industrial control systems, and consumer products.

A *microprocessor* is an LSI chip that is capable of performing arithmetic and logical functions under program control in a bit-parallel fashion. A microprocessor alone is not an operational computer—additional circuits for memory and input/output must be supplied and interfaced with the system, as well as the software for controlling the operation of the microprocessor itself. The design and development of such a *microcomputer* from a microprocessor and other integrated circuit components form the basic subject matter of this book.

This book is an introduction to the technology, architecture, and applications of microprocessors and microcomputers. It is directed to the potential user of microprocessors—the electronic designer or computer systems analyst who is planning to incorporate a microprocessor in a specific application.

The first chapter is a review of basic computer architecture that is relevant to microcomputer system design. Chapter 2 considers the basic tasks of microcomputer system design and summarizes the essential components of a microcomputer.

The third chapter presents the basic semiconductor technology of microprocessor manufacture. Although the details of semiconductor process technology are not of direct interest to the microcomputer system designer, the physical operating characteristics and cost of microprocessors are based on such considerations. A knowledge of the basic bipolar and MOS technologies used in the fabrication of microprocessors gives the user a greater appreciation of the capabilities and limitations of the devices.

Chapter 4 is a survey of the architecture of a variety of commercially available microprocessors. With new microprocessors being announced every few months, and older microprocessors becoming obsolete, the survey is merely designed to illustrate the wide range of capabilities and architectures that may be found in commercially available microprocessors.

Chapter 5 is a summary of the operation of one of the more popular microprocessors—the Intel 8080. The instruction set, the timing and synchronization, and the operation of the internal registers are typical of many other microprocessors.

Microprocessor programming is somewhat different from regular computer programming, since greater attention must be paid to system hardware components. Chapter 6 covers the topic of system definition flowcharts, coding, and testing and debugging. Microprocessor development systems, important tools for designing and developing a prototype microcomputer system, are reviewed in Chapter 7.

A consideration of potential applications for microprocessors is presented in Chapters 8 and 9, ranging from simple home microcomputer applications to more sophisticated telecommunications examples.

DANIEL R. MCGLYNN

Briarcliff Manor,
New York
January 1976

CONTENTS

CHAPTER FIVE
MICROPROCESSOR OPERATION   101

CHAPTER SIX
MICROPROCESSOR PROGRAMMING   125

CHAPTER SEVEN
MICROPROCESSOR DEVELOPMENT SYSTEMS   142

CHAPTER EIGHT
MICROPROCESSOR APPLICATIONS   149

CHAPTER NINE
ADVANCED MICROPROCESSOR APPLICATIONS   162

MICROPROCESSORS

CHAPTER ONE
INTRODUCTION TO MICROCOMPUTERS

A microcomputer is a stored-program computer that utilizes a microprocessor as the central processing unit of the system. Before we describe microprocessors and microcomputer systems in greater detail, it would be useful to first briefly review the fundamental concepts of digital computer technology—hardware architecture, software, and operating systems.

The most general representation of a digital computer consists of four basic units: input/output, memory, arithmetic/logic circuits, and control. All general-purpose computers, from microcomputers to large-scale multiprocessing systems, can be described in terms of these basic units. The particular design and interrelation between these four units are called the "architecture" of the machine.

Computer architecture encompasses both hardware and software structures and describes the interaction between the static hardware design and the dynamic software processing. Although there are numerous types and classifications of computer architectures, we only consider the two most practical architectures here for microcomputer applications:

von Neumann architecture
stack architecture

After examining these architectures in detail, we indicate how they may be implemented in microcomputer systems and present some of the more important economic issues raised by microprocessor technology.

COMPUTER ARCHITECTURE

The four basic architectural units of a general purpose digital computer are shown in a simplified block diagram in Fig. 1.1. A general-purpose computer is an information-processing device that performs a series of arithmetic or logical operations on supplied information. Information is transferred in and out of the computer by means of input/output (or I/O) devices. Inside the computer, both the information to be processed and

1

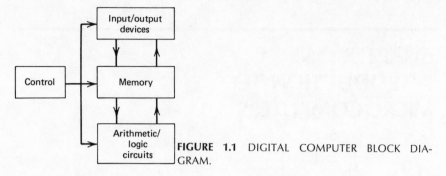

FIGURE 1.1 DIGITAL COMPUTER BLOCK DIAGRAM.

the encoded operations to be performed on the information are stored in a memory. The actual processing is done by digital logic circuits that are clocked and sequenced by a control unit. The control unit also coordinates operation of the I/O devices and the memory with the arithmetic/logic circuits.

The different types of computer architectures arise from variations on this simplified functional block structure. These variations arise from increasing the number of memories or arithmetic/logical circuits (processors), or by specifying the nature of the control exercised between the basic units. More sophisticated architectures may define hierarchical levels of memories and processors and establish strict system control procedures for optimizing use of a scarce system resource. Although such architectures may be, and probably at some time will be, implemented using microprocessors, present applications of microcomputer systems do not require such sophisticated design.

von Neumann Architecture

The von Neumann type architecture is the most commonly used in digital computers and is the basis for almost all microprocessor architectures. The von Neumann architecture specifies the type of interaction between the control and the memory. The control section operates on the basis of a sequence of instructions called a *program* which is stored in memory. Each instruction consists of two parts: an *operator* and an *operand* (Fig. 1.2). The operator specifies the specific operation to be performed by the processor (arithmetic operations like ADD, logical operations like AND, or control operations like JUMP) while the operand specifies the data or address in memory to be operated upon.

The von Neumann computer operates by executing a sequence of instructions that correspond to the operations to be performed by the system.

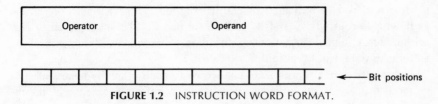

FIGURE 1.2 INSTRUCTION WORD FORMAT.

Since there is considerable interaction between the control unit and the memory, special hardware structures, shown in Fig. 1.3, are provided to expedite the data and instruction transfers. These hardware structures are:

instruction register
program counter
accumulator
arithmetic/logic unit (ALU)

The instruction register, program counter, and accumulator are the most fundamental elements of the "memory" basic building block of Fig. 1.1. These elements are *registers,* or storage cells typically having a capacity in bits equal to the word length of the machine. The instruction register stores the next instruction to be executed by the computer. The program counter stores the location in memory of the next subsequent instruction to be executed by the computer. The accumulator stores data that are to be processed or accepts new data after being processed.

The ALU performs the specified arithmetic or logical calculations on

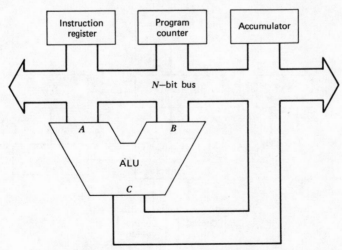

FIGURE 1.3 BIDIRECTIONAL BUS ARCHITECTURE.

predetermined data indicated by the instruction. The ALU is represented as having two inputs A and B, and an output C. The ALU executes the arithmetic or logical operation on the data provided on inputs A and B, and places the result on output C.

These hardware structures are connected to each other by means of one or more *busses*. A bus is an electrical connection between several points which may act as sources or sinks for signals. (One should compare the vehicular analogy of passengers getting on and off at different stops). In the representation shown in Fig. 1.3 there is a single bidirectional bus which is *n* bits wide, where *n* is the word length of the machine. Microcomputer word lengths are typically 4, 8, or 16 bits.

The bus connects these registers and the ALU with memory and the I/O devices. In a single-bus architecture, each device tied to the bus shares the bus with the other devices and so is allocated a specific time slot in which to convey information to another device along the bus or receive information from another device. This time multiplexing of the bus is handled by bus control hardware and synchronized by the control unit of the computer.

The control unit performs the basic supervision and synchronization of all other units of the computer. Computer systems are typically synchronous sequential digital circuits. They are synchronized on the basis of a standard clock signal that is provided throughout the system. Each computer element is designed to make a sequential transition after a predetermined number of clock pulses.

Figure 1.4 is a simplified representation of the basic elements of a von

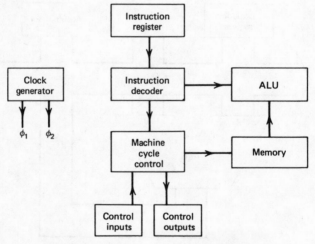

FIGURE 1.4   VON NEUMANN ARCHITECTURE.

Neumann computer. A clock generator is shown having two output phases ϕ_1 and ϕ_2. The basic operative element of the computer is the ALU, which was discussed in connection with Fig. 1.3. The instruction register provides the next instruction to the instruction decoder, which interprets the bit pattern to supply appropriate instruction indications to both the machine cycle control and the ALU. The machine cycle control unit decodes such indications to provide external indications of the type of instruction being executed through control outputs, as well as the memory. Thus other system components can be synchronized with the operation of the ALU. The memory, which may be read/write memory or an internal machine register, must also be signaled to indicate which data are to be supplied for processing. Finally, various control inputs are shown for providing external control of machine cycles, such as for a halt or interrupt operation.

Stack Architecture

The architecture of a computer may also be organized around the user language in which it is programmed. There are numerous variations of such architectures, called "reconfigurable architectures" or "compilable architectures," which are expected to be important areas of application of microprocessors in the future. At present, however, the most commercially significant of these architectures is "stack architecture," so-called because of the use of last-in first-out stacks for handling system information.

Stack architecture was developed in the early 1960s to increase the effectiveness of computation by providing a means for the direct execution of instructions—the stack. A stack is merely a temporary storage facility, either a separate buffer memory, or a specific portion of the main memory, that operates to store information in sequence. As new information is entered into the stack, other information already in the stack is "moved down" in the stack. As information is removed from the stack, the information is "removed up" in reverse order. Thus the last information placed in the top of the stack is the first information out. This concept of a last-in first-out pushdown stack is more graphically illustrated in Fig. 1.5, where "push" refers to the process of entering information into the stack, while "pop" refers to removing information from the stack.

The representation of a stack as depicted in Fig. 1.5 is merely meant to indicate how stack operations occur, and is not a representation of how a last-in first-out stack is actually implemented in a computer. Although it appears functionally that memory data are "pushed down" or "popped up" in a stack, the actual operation is quite different.

Figure 1.6 shows how a stack is actually formed in memory. The key element is the *stack pointer,* which is a register that contains the address

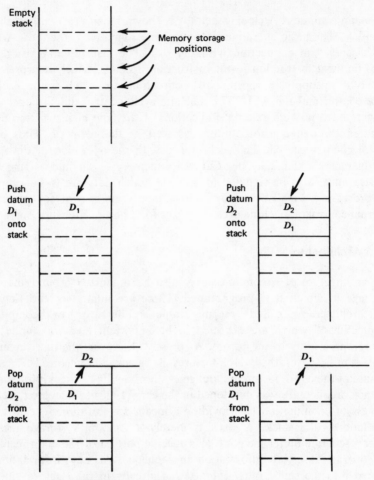

FIGURE 1.5   PUSHDOWN STACK OPERATION.

of the memory location that is considered to be the "top" of the stack. The top representation of Fig. 1.6 shows the stack pointer containing the address 051. The contents of memory location 051 is the datum D1. When a datum D2 is "pushed" onto the stack, it enters location 050. The stack pointer is then revised to read 050, which represents the new location of the top of the stack, as shown in the bottom representation of Fig. 1.6.

Correspondingly, when data are "popped" from the stack, they are read out of the memory location to which the stack pointer points, and the stack pointer is incremented by one.

The "memory" to which the stack pointer refers may be either the main memory of the computer, or a higher speed buffer memory. Both of these implementations are available in microprocessor systems.

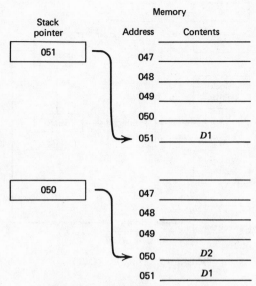

FIGURE 1.6   STACK IMPLEMENTATION.

Although stacks may be implemented in a computer system based on a von Neumann architecture, as is the case with many microprocessor systems to enhance their computational facilities, they are the fundamental operational structure in the *stack processor,* a computer designed around stack architecture.

Stack Processors.   Stack processors are utilized to more efficiently execute higher level language code. This particular method utilizes a particular format or presentation of data and instruction code for execution by the computer. This format is known as Polish notation and may be represented by a number of variations, known as Polish prefix, Polish postfix, and reverse Polish notation.

In the stack machine, the compiler performs the required syntactical and semantic analysis of the code and represents the program as a sequence of machine operations. The Polish postfix notation has actually been implemented in the Burroughs B-5500 and B-6500 machines, as well as the English Electric KDF-9.

It would be worthwhile to discuss the actual stack implementation in the B-6500 here as an example of a particular implementation of a stack architecture. The hardware structure of a stack processor is illustrated in Fig. 1.7. A standard Memory and a Memory Address Register (MAR) are provided in a stack processor similar to those in the von Neumann machine.

The data and control statements are referred to as "syllables" in a stack

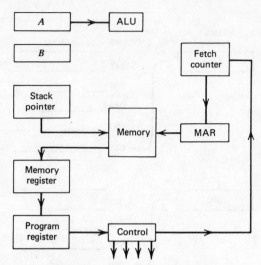

FIGURE 1.7   STACK PROCESSOR.

processor, to distinguish them from "instructions" in a von Neumann machine. There are three basic types of syllables:

operator syllables
value call syllables
literal syllables

The operator syllables express the specific arithmetic or logical operations to be performed by the processor. The value call syllables indicate the memory address where the desired operands are located. The literal syllables are the actual operands.

A program for execution by a stack processor consists simply of a sequence of syllables that represent the arithmetic or logical operation to be performed in Polish notation. These syllables are stored in memory in consecutive memory locations. The address of the first program syllable in memory is set in the Fetch Counter. In response to an internal control pulse, the Fetch Counter signals the Memory Address Register to transfer the specified program syllable out of Memory.

As the program syllable is transferred out of Memory, the Fetch Counter is incremented, and the program syllable is stored in a Memory Register. From the Memory Register the program syllable is transferred to a Program Register where the syllable is decoded. The syllable is typically provided with a two-bit field that designates whether the syllable is an operator, value call, or literal syllable. Once the syllable in the Program Register is decoded, a specific sequence of control pulses are sent to other components of the system for synchronizing them for the performance of operation designated by the decoded syllable.

The subsequence control operations as well as the stack mechanism can be more easily explained with reference to a simple example. Consider the problem of evaluating the following arithmetic expression:

$$x = (a+b) / (c-d)$$

for a given set of integer values of $a, b, c,$ and d.

The first task is to express the standard arithmetic expression above in parenthesis-free Polish notation. Although any form of Polish notation may be used, the postfix notation has been generally adopted for the commercially available computers. In postfix notation the operators (e.g., add and subtract) are written to the *right* of a pair of operands. In postfix notation the arithmetic expression above becomes:

$$ab+cd-/$$

The rules for operating on an expression or string of this nature in Polish postfix notation are as follows:

1. Scan the string from left to right.
2. Remember the operands and the order in which they occur.
3. When an operator is encountered do the following:
    a. Take the two operands that are last in order.
    b. Operate on them according to the type of operator encountered.
    c. Eliminate these two operands from further consideration.
    d. Remember the result of step b and consider it as the last operand in order.

Another way of representing a Polish Notation string is by means of a binary tree. Instead of the operating rules being applied left-to-right to a string, they now would apply to the sequence of branches. The binary tree form shown in Fig. 1.8 more pictorially represents the precedence and sequence of operators.

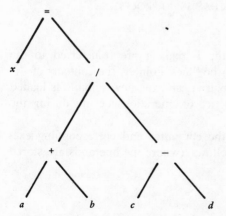

FIGURE 1.8 BINARY TREE.

These operations are performed using the stack mechanism of the processor. These hardware elements of the processor shown in Fig. 1.7 refer to the stack mechanism: the A register, the B register, and the Stack Pointer. The A register represents the top of the stack, the B register is the level immediately below the A register level, and the Stack Pointer points to the address in Memory that represents the next lower level. A pictorial representation of the stack is shown in Fig. 1.9.

The "push" and "pop" operations of the stack defined by the A and B registers and memory are the same as those of any last-in first-out stack. When a new syllable is added to the top of the stack, the Stack Pointer

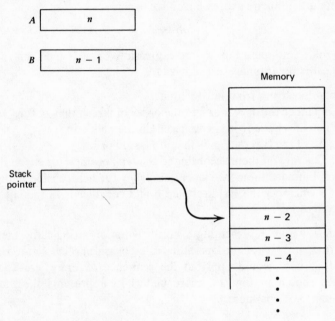

FIGURE 1.9   STACK MECHANISM IN PROCESSOR.

advances by one, the contents of the B register are transferred to the memory position now referenced by the Stack Pointer, the contents of the A register are transferred to the B register, and the new syllable is loaded in the A register. The reverse sequence of operations occurs during the "pop" operation.

The syllable string program for the computer and corresponding execution action using the stack is as follows (where the operands are stored in memory) :

Program	Action	Contents of stack	
1...Value call for a...	a→Stack...	a)	
2...Value call for b...	b→Stack...	ab)	
3...Add operator...	$a+b=r_1$...	r_1)	Top of
4...Value call for c...	c→Stack...	r_1c)	the stack
5...Value call for d...	d→Stack...	r_1cd)	
6...Subtract operator...	$c-d=r_2$...	r_1r_2)	
7...Divide operator...	$r_1/r_2=r_3$...	r_3)	

The result of the execution is thus placed at the top of the stack, in the A register, where it may be utilized in subsequent operations or provided on an output from the processor.

The execution of more complex programs on a stack processor is an iteration of this basic stack formation and processing technique. A stack processor is particularly adapted to executing a "block structured" language, such as ALGOL, COBOL, or PL/1.

In a block-structured language, the various procedures to be executed are broken up into a hierarchical structure of independent blocks, and subblocks within blocks, such as shown in Fig. 1.10.

Each block refers to a particular procedure that is to be executed by the program. Distinctions are made between blocks with regard to the types of parameters and variables that may be defined therein. The basic rule is that a parameter or variable may be referred to in a block only if it is "local" or "global" with respect to that block.

A parameter or variable that is defined or "declared" within a particular block is said to be "local" with respect to that block. A parameter or

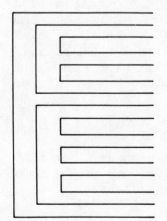

FIGURE 1.10 BLOCK STRUCTURED LANGUAGE.

variable is "global" with respect to a particular block if that block is a subblock to a block in which the parameter or variable is defined.

Parameters or variables may then be characterized by two parameters: the lexicographical level of the block or procedure in which it is declared, and the index or displacement used to locate the variable within the particular block or procedure in which it is declared. The address of a variable therefore includes these two pieces of information: the lexicographical level L of the block or procedure in which it is declared, and the index or displacement D used to locate the variable within this specific or particular block or procedure. A set of display cells or registers act as pointers to the stack section that is referenced. Local variables are then addressed relative to these pointers; that is, L specifies a point in the stack, and D gives a displacement from this point. The basic feature is that the display pointers provide the addressing environment in which an address couple (L, D) is to be interpreted by the system.

A block-structured language, such as ALGOL, is easy to implement on a data-processing system including a stack mechanism. The stacks contain storage areas for each ALGOL block. Each block storage area of a particular stack has associated with it a marked stack control word (MSCW). The MSCW serves to identify the particular block storage area of a stack. Particular data within the block storage area may then be referenced by relative addressing with respect to the location of the corresponding MSCW. The display registers point to the MSCW for each block storage area.

The stack mechanism in a data-processing system serves two additional functions. The first function is that it provides a means for the temporary storage of parameters and references to data and program segments. A second function is that it provides a means to store an indication of the history of the program. This is achieved by the programming feature of providing two lists in memory. The first list is a stack history list, which refers to the actual sequential order in which a stack is filled. The second list is an addressing environment list, which refers to the sequential ordering of the block storage areas according to the block structure rules of the higher level language used, such as ALGOL.

MICROPROCESSOR ARCHITECTURE

As a central processing unit, a microprocessor has the same basic architecture as a larger scale computer. The basic functional building blocks of a microprocessor are:

   an arithmetic/logic unit

instruction decoder
control and synchronization

These basic building blocks are presented in a highly simplified block diagram of a typical microprocessor architecture in Fig. 1.11. Making reference to these basic building blocks, a microprocessor may be defined as an IC component that is capable of performing arithmetical and logical operations under program control in a bit-parallel fashion.

Before elaborating on this definition and the accompanying block diagram a word of caution is necessary. Microprocessors date from about 1971, and since that time the term microprocessor has generally referred to the "computer-on-a-chip" concept defined above. Prior to 1971, and in a few isolated instances afterwards, the term microprocessor had a different meaning. Before 1971, a microprocessor was a processor that executed microinstructions; that is, a processor that was microprogrammed. This alternate and outdated use of the term microprocessor appeared particularly in the academic literature. Since 1971, the term microprocessor, both in the academic literature and in the trade press, has referred to an IC "computer-on-a-chip."

For completeness, it should also be noted that one of the world's leading general purpose computer manufacturers has announced products which contain "microprocessors." The company defines such "microprocessors" as advanced large-scale-integrated devices with speeds and densities rela-

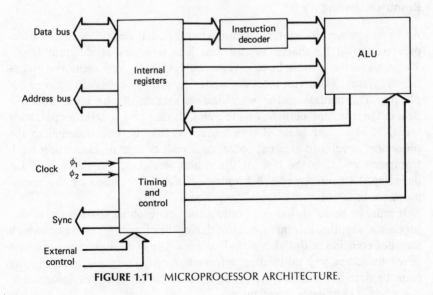

FIGURE 1.11 MICROPROCESSOR ARCHITECTURE.

tively comparable to single-chip central-processor-unit devices available from the major semiconductor component manufacturers.

Returning now to the present day definition of microprocessor, an explanation of the function of the basic building blocks is made with reference to Fig. 1.11. The ALU, as the name implies, performs basic arithmetic and logical operations on binary data stored in two registers of the microprocessor. Such operations are performed by an *adder* as well as Boolean *logic gates*. The instruction decoder is typically an internal read-only memory which translates the machine instruction code into microinstructions which are executed by the processor. Some microprocessors permit the user to define these microinstructions on an external control read-only memory chip. The control and synchronization block interprets the microinstructions to put out appropriate control and synchronization pulses to other parts of the system.

Microprocessors generally use busses as a means for transferring data, addresses, and control signals between system components. The reason is that microprocessors are packaged as conveniently as practical, which means IC packages having a minimum number of pins.

A number of other architectural features of microprocessors should also be noted here:

    resource sharing
    memory access and transfer
    interrupts

Resource Sharing

As in any computer system, a number of scarce resources in a microprocessor must be shared by different jobs or users at different times. These resources include busses, registers, I/O pins, and memory or control programs. These resources are shared by means of time-division multiplexing. The control and synchronization section of the microprocessor defines specific time periods, or subcycles, during which certain operations are allowed to take place. These operations may be both internal to the processor, or refer to external operations, such as data or instruction fetch from memory. It is the task of the system design to provide means for decoding the control and synchronization signals provided by the microprocessor to coordinate external operations.

It must be realized that as a consequence of resource sharing the microprocessor supplies information only during brief periods of time, which may not coincide with those periods when other system elements are prepared to accept and utilize that information. Auxiliary hardware, in the form of decoders and latches, must be used to capture this information and apply it to other system elements.

Resource sharing and its consequential impact on microcomputer system design are results of the temporal architecture of microprocessors. This architecture, as represented by the timing diagram, is presented in greater detail later with specific reference to particular microprocessors.

Memory Access and Transfer

Memory access and transfer architecture are other important features that are critical for certain system design applications. High-speed operations, particularly requiring considerable data transfer between memory and peripheral devices, utilize the memory access arrangement known as Direct Memory Access (DMA). DMA is the direct transfer of data from or to predetermined memory locations to or from a peripheral device without direct processor control. DMA is implemented by means of an external bus that connects the external random access memory, the peripherals, and the microprocessor. When the microprocessor is not using the external bus, external hardware may be activated to affect a data transfer along the bus between the peripheral device and memory.

The amount of data to be transferred by DMA is first specified in some manner, such as by a counter in memory. The starting and ending addresses are also indicated by external hardware. The only remaining task is to determine when the external bus is free for the transfer.

A microprocessor, like a larger scale digital computer, operates on the basis of synchronous sequential circuits. The processor performs certain operations during predetermined clock cycles, for example, reading and writing operations that utilize the external bus. During other clock cycles, the processor performs internal operations, thereby freeing the bus for use by the peripherals and memory. The specific times during which the bus is free is indicated by the synchronization and state information that is obtainable from the microprocessor. By decoding the synchronization and state information, an indication that the bus is free for use may be transferred to the peripherals and memory. The peripheral device then "cycle steals" from the processor and transfers the data along the bus to the memory during the unused processor cycle time. This concept of cycle stealing is a very important one for efficient microprocessor system design using high-speed peripherals.

Interrupts

Certain applications of microcomputer systems require immediate response of the processor to an external condition. In such cases the processor must interrupt the program presently being executed and begin a new program to handle the external condition or *interrupt*. There are a number of different types of interrupts depending on the number and priority of external devices to be serviced.

simple interrupt
vectored interrupt
priority interrupt

The simple interrupt merely specifies that a single external device requires servicing by the processor. The vectored interrupt provides the facility to recognize an interrupt from any one of several external devices. More particularly, the vectored interrupt specifies which device requires servicing. This specification is done by a data field, or "vector," which specifies the identity of the external device. Finally, a priority interrupt also recognizes an interrupt from any one of several external devices, but specifies which device has priority over other devices. Such priority or multiple-level processing is available only on a few microprocessors.

The presence of an external condition, such as an "interrupt request," is indicated to the timing and control section of the microprocessor by means of external control lines which couple with predetermined pins of the chip. The timing and control section responds to such external control signals to performing the appropriate resetting and saving operations for handling the interrupt routine.

MICROPROCESSOR SOFTWARE

A microprocessor operates by means of a sequence of instructions which constitute the "software," as opposed to the physical hardware on which the instructions are executed. Software, or machine instructions, are essentially replacements of hardware components: instead of using two particular hardware components, for example, an instruction will specify that the operation be performed twice on a single component. Once the basic logical functions are supplied in hardware, any arithmetic or logical calculation may be done by a program of instructions.

The use of microprocessor software as a replacement for hardware components is one of the key advantages of microprocessor systems. Any hardware arrangement can be modeled or simulated by software, and implemented in a microprocessor system. Cost considerations that make a hardware design impractical for a given application are not applicable to software design, and as noted in a later section, many current microprocessor applications consist of the replacement of high-cost random-logic hardware systems by a lower cost programmed microprocessor system.

The trade-offs between software and hardware implementations for a given processing function depend on the specific application and related economic factors that are analyzed in greater detail in the next chapter. What should be realized here is that a microprocessor system has built-in software capabilities which should be realized in its particular application.

It is possible, however, to quantify the trade-off between hardware and software. If we assume that one hardware gate (such as NAND or NOR) is equivalent to one or two instructions, then we can compare the number of IC chips necessary for a given application versus the number of instructions. Using a rough yardstick that the average IC contains about 10 gates, we calculate that a system program that occupies 2 Kbits (i.e. 2048 bits) in a read-only memory would replace 128 to 256 gates, or 13 to 25 ICs.

This calculation applies to machines with an 8-bit instruction word length. Of course it must be realized that hardware and software are not directly interchangeable, and each has its own characteristic overheads that would not be accounted for in a rough calculation. However, for the purpose of a simplified comparison between hardware and software, the yardsticks above are reasonable and the conclusions one could draw from them would be valid.

The advantage of software over hardware is that it is a nonrecurring cost item. Once the software for a system has been designed and tested, it can be duplicated and stored in memory of any number of systems. Thus the total development cost for the software is spread over the total system production. Hardware, which must be duplicated in every system, is a recurring cost item. Even though the cost of ICs themselves may be small, each system must be assembled and tested, which may amount to considerable expense if there are complex arrays.

As noted above, software is the sequence of instructions that control the operation of the microcomputer. In the typical microcomputer system, a number of basic programs perform the essential system operations. Unlike in large-scale computers, it is impractical to load these programs from external storage every time the machine is turned on. Microcomputers store these frequently used control programs permanently in a read-only memory (ROM) chip. Thus modification of the program is achieved by merely replacing the ROM IC with another ROM IC which contains different control programs. This feature of microprocessor system design is one of the most significant advantages of such software implementation in a microcomputer system.

There are a number of different levels of software which we should consider:

system executive
programs
subroutines
microprograms

The *system executive* is concerned with overall job, task, and data management for the system. In particular, the executive defines and controls the mode of operation of the computer system. The various modes of computer operation are:

dedicated operation
batch processing
interactive processing
time-sharing
concurrent

Depending on the complexity of the system executive, the microcomputer may operate in any, some, or all of these modes of operation. In larger scale computer systems, the system executive may be called the *monitor, supervisor,* or *operating system.*

A *program* is a set of instructions for performing a specific operation or function. A program often consists of a discrete number of individual *routines* or *subroutines* which perform a specific calculation or algorithm.

Some routines are so basic or are used so often that it is frequently worthwhile to encode such routines as *microinstructions* in a microprogrammable computer. A single complex user instruction is translated into a sequence of simpler microinstructions which directly control the hardware operation.

A number of microprocessors are in fact microprogrammable. A brief discussion of microprogramming is present in Chapter 6, and the microprogrammable features of a few microprocessors are noted in Chapter 4.

MINICOMPUTERS AND MICROCOMPUTERS

The microcomputer is more than just structurally different from larger scale computers or minicomputers, it is an entirely new concept in data processing. To begin with, a microprocessor is a component, merely one element of a microcomputer system. As a component, it makes possible entirely new areas of application of stored-program computers that were impractical for reasons of cost, size, or design reasons. Some of these applications are listed in the next section, and Chapters 8 and 9 describe the system architecture of a few of the more important applications in greater detail. However, it must be emphasized that the greatest potential area of application for microcomputers are those areas that were believed impractical for minicomputers or hardwired logic.

Perhaps the best way to characterize the difference between microprocessor systems and minicomputer or hardwired logic systems is to consider the feasibility of an electronic system as a funtion of two parameters—the complexity of the system and the number of units expected to be produced. Figure 1.12 is a representation of the relative suitability of various system designs as a function of these two parameters. For low-volume applications, requiring a relatively sophisticated computational capability, standard minicomputers are probably the most practical approach. On the other extreme, in high-volume operations, the use of custom LSI circuits, even custom microprocessors, is most cost-effective. Microprocessor systems find application somewhere between these two extremes—in moderate volume production systems, with medium levels of complexity.

To a great extent, microprocessors and microcomputer systems are not directly competitive with minicomputers, since their markets are essentially different. Although there may be some overlap in applications that may be implemented by microprocessors and minicomputers, their method of implementation is totally different.

As we noted above, a microprocessor is a component just like any other IC or electronic component. It is sold off the shelf with a specification sheet and maybe an applications manual, together with the best wishes of a manufacturer's representative.

On the other hand, a minicomputer is now sold as a solution to a problem, rather than as a piece of hardware, by the trained sales and applica-

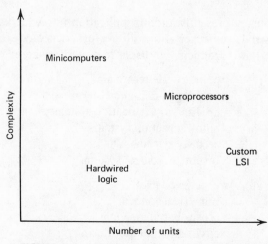

FIGURE 1.12   SYSTEM DESIGN ALTERNATIVES.

tions engineering staff of the minicomputer manufacturers. Minicomputer manufacturers supply a system, rather than merely a computer. The system includes peripherals, software, support, and maintenance. The purchaser of a minicomputer system does not need to know anything about computers or programming and may rely totally on the manufacturer to design, install, and maintain the system.

The manufacturers of microprocessors are semiconductor component houses. They are in the business of producing electronic components for originial equipment manufacturers (OEM), rather than the end user. The development of the microprocessor, a product particularly suitable for customized user adaptation, is a good case study of a product appearing before there was a market for it.

Not surprisingly, the implementation of microprocessors in products has been slow. Although users who had experience with digital logic were able to develop microprocessor implementations of their product, many other manufacturers found such development a long and expensive learning process.

Microprocessor manufacturers realize that the burden is on them to address themselves to the user market, and the development of software, prototype kits, training courses, and other aids are a first step in this direction. Microprocessors are now at the stage of development that the minicomputer was in the mid-1960s, and in a few years it is expected that the microprocessor industry will reach a stage of development and importance similar to that of the minicomputer industry today.

MICROPROCESSOR APPLICATIONS AND IMPACTS

Microprocessors are presently finding application in a wide variety of commercial, industrial, consumer, and military products. As examples of the wide range of these products, we list a few of them here:

Commercial: point-of-sale terminals
                   banking and financial terminals
                   credit card verification systems
                   autotransaction systems
                   security systems
                   inventory control systems

Industrial: process control
                   numerical control
                   sensor-based systems
                   environmental monitoring
                   data acquisition systems

Consumer:	home microcomputer
	educational systems
	intelligent toys and games
	programmable appliances
	automotive monitoring and control
Military:	communications
	navigation systems
	simulators and training equipment
Instrumentation:	automatic test equipment
	electronic instruments
	analytical chemical and medical equipment
Communications:	remote terminals
	programmable controllers
	switching systems
	multiplexers
	message handling
	error detection
Data Processing:	programmable calculators
	office computers
	peripheral processors
	I/O controllers
	communications interface
	performance monitoring
	auditing and security

This spectrum of applications may be represented in terms of the complexity of the system and the anticipated volume in Fig. 1.13.

In addition to their application in numerous products, microprocessors are expected to have important impacts on a number of industries. The three most important industries to be affected are the electronics industry, the mini- or small business computer industry, and the large-scale data-processing industry.

The development of microprocessors may have been an evolutionary step in the semiconductor component industry, but it is a revolutionary step in the data processing, instrumentation, and industrial control field. By "revolutionary" we mean to imply a fundamental change in the structure of an industry. Since the microprocessor revolution is in its early stages, it is somewhat difficult to detect these changes from a contemporary vantage point; however we will point out trends marking these changes due to the impact of microprocessors in these various industries noted below.

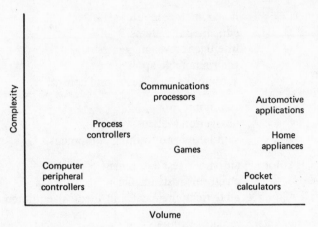

FIGURE 1.13 APPLICATIONS SPECTRUM.

Impact on the Electronics Industry

The first and most important impact of microprocessors is in the electronics industry. Sophisticated digital electronics products, such as instruments, communications devices, process control equipment, and the like use considerable amounts of digital hardware in the form of IC components hardwired together to form a processor for performing a specific sequence of arithmetic or logical functions. Such hardware may now be replaced by software operating a single microprocessor. There are several advantages in replacing hardware by a programmed microprocessor:

1. Lower Cost—by replacing hardware by software one replaces a recurring cost item (the IC hardware found in the final product) by a noncurring cost item (the software that is merely a list of instructions to be performed by the processor).

2. Reliability—by eliminating the hardware components needed to do the processing, one reduces the number of discrete parts in the system.

3. Flexibility—the software program for the system is contained in a replaceable memory chip; if the system should be modified for some reason, such as to accept data in a different format, the user need only write a new program and replace a single plug-in IC that contains the program; such flexibility is impractical with a hard-wired system.

More important are those electronic products which are now economically feasible using microprocessors. Such products, in instrumentation, consumer products, or industrial control, define entirely new markets, and create a fundamental change in the structure of numerous industries traditionally serving such markets.

Impact on Mini and Small Business Computers

The second most significant impact of the microprocessor is expected to be on the minicomputer and small business computer manufacturers. Although the mini and the small business computer are market-defined products, the technology of these products have important competitive ramifications. The economy, size, and adaptability of the microprocessor make them particularly suitable in the small-scale computer system.

The small business computer (typified by IBM's System/32, Burroughs B700, DEC's Datasystem 300, Basic/Four, and others) is a good example of a potential application of the microprocessor. Such products do not require the speed, versatile instruction capabilities, or large data bases associated with large-scale computer systems. One such small business computer, the Q1/LMC manufactured by Q1 Corporation of Farmingdale, New York, uses the Intel 8008 microprocessor. The Q1 system, selling for less than $25,000, is a low-cost accounting and financial-oriented machine that is particularly popular for credit union applications.

The minicomputer is also expected to emerge as another potential application. Minicomputers are now manufactured from hardwired ICs which are organized on a couple of printed circuit boards. By replacing these ICs with a microprocessor there is considerable savings in size and cost. Of course the success of the minicomputer is based on the support software and user programs that have taken many years to develop. Therefore the strategy of minicomputer manufacturers is to have microprocessor chips developed which can execute already existing manufacturer's and user's software. Digital Equipment Corporation is in fact doing this for its PDP-11 minicomputer: Western Digital Corp. has developed a three chip N-channel MOS technology microprocessor designed to emulate the instruction set of the PDP-11.

Impact on the Data-Processing Industry

Perhaps the least noticeably impact of microprocessors will be on the large-scale data-processing industry. The impact of microprocessors is expected to be focused in two directions:

extremely lost cost of simple processing functions
size and simplicity of processor elements, making possible new system architectures

The first point is demonstrated by the price/performance trend diagram shown in Fig. 1.14.

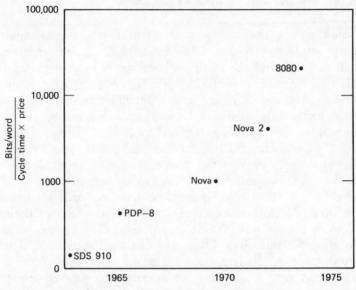

FIGURE 1.14   PRICE/PERFORMANCE TREND.

The decreased price/performance of the microprocessor (typified by the 8080 shown on the diagram above) compared to minicomputers opens up several new areas of applications, both in small business computers as noted in the previous section, and in intelligent peripherals for large-scale data-processing systems.

The size of microprocessors is also expected to have significant impact on the system architecture of the large-scale computer systems of the future. By reducing processor size, it is possible to distribute such processing functions closer to the user. Such distributed processing systems include "autotransaction" systems for supermarkets, retail stores, and financial industry applications. Such intelligent terminals are expected to account for one-third of all computer industry revenues by 1980 according to a recent study.

Outlook

Microprocessors are going to have a significant impact on almost all industries in the next 5 to 10 years. As a high-volume, low-cost product, it will not be surprising to see the following trends emerge as shaping the future microcomputer industry:

increasing product differentiation and market segmentation.
elimination or consolidation of directly competing products.

    development of "pin-to-pin" compatible ICs and peripheral support
      hardware.

    increased emphasis on software rather than hardware development.

    displacement of certain minicomputer and hardwired logic applications.

    adaptation and integration of microprocessors into fourth generation
      large scale computer systems.

    redesign of products and systems as digital rather than analog, and per-
      forming digital operations under program control.

In conclusion, it is believed that the microprocessor is one of the most significant technological advances in recent years and should have a major influence in the economics and design characteristics of systems in the electronics and data processing industries.

CHAPTER TWO
MICROCOMPUTER
SYSTEMS DESIGN

Microcomputer systems design is the task of designing and developing a microcomputer for specific applications from a microprocessor and other component elements. The basic elements that comprise a microcomputer are:

microprocessor
random-access memory (RAM)
read-only memory (ROM)
input/output devices (I/O)
interface components

In addition to developing the hardware for the microcomputer, the system designer must also develop the software—both the executive control program for managing the microcomputer system, and the functional programs for performing the desired tasks and operations. The specification and selection of specific hardware components are covered in the present chapter, while software design, programming, and programming aids such as development systems are treated later in this book.

A microcomputer or microprocessor system is not typically designed as a general-purpose computer or minicomputer but is developed for a particular application or operating environment. Microprocessor system architecture, component selection, and even software are not intended to handle a large number of different applications, but rather a small number of applications in the most expedient manner.

Before turning to an analysis of the basic elements of the microcomputer, the fundamental tasks of the system designer in developing a microcomputer system should be reviewed:

establishing system design criteria
determining whether a microprocessor system is feasible
selecting the microprocessor
designing the auxiliary hardware
developing software

integrating hardware and software
debugging and testing
developing maintenance facilities

SYSTEM DESIGN CRITERIA

The first step in microcomputer system design is to develop a set of criteria for system design and component selection with the intended applications in mind. Some of these criteria are:

cost
flexibility
compatibility
reliability
speed
size

In commercial applications, *cost* of the system is one of the principal considerations. However, unlike a minicomputer system, the cost of implementing a microprocessor system cannot be precisely determined before actually constructing the system. The reason is simply that the cost of system design and programming is a much more important factor than the cost of the hardware alone for the first prototype system. The cost of system design and programming depends on the experience and cost of the technical staff, as well as the complexity of the design itself.

It must be emphasized that a microprocessor is merely a component. Its inherent cost advantages over other types of digital systems are not realized unless a sizable number of identical systems are produced. Since system design and programming are one-time expenses, the greater the number of systems, the lower the per-unit design and programming cost.

System *flexibility* is another key advantage of a microprocessor based system. The flexibility is based on the replacement of hardware by software in a microprocessor system. If, after finalization of a design or installation of a system, the customer requires a system modification to accept new data or perform new functions, it is quite possible that the required modification can be implemented by changing the software alone. No hardware changes would normally be necessary. The software modification is also simple to implement. Once a new program is written and tested, a new ROM may be prepared to replace the ROM in the system containing the obsolete program. By a simple physical replacement of the ROM package, the user has reprogrammed the system without any hardware circuit modifications.

System *compatibility* is a much broader issue. At the present stage of industry development, there is in fact little compatibility between a microprocessor based computer system and any other data processing system. Interfaces must be custom designed for every application. And each microprocessor has its own architecture and language so that no two microprocessor systems are compatible with each other.

It must be realized that the system designer designing a microprocessor based system is in fact developing a new computer having general-purpose capabilities. Compatibility within the system itself is the object of the design, rather than attempting to make the system compatible with an external system.

The use of microprogramming in many of the microprocessors makes the design of compatibility particularly simple, as is pointed out in a later chapter.

Reliability is another important reason for selecting microprocessor based systems. The smaller number of components makes assembly and testing of units relatively simple, as well as making replacement of defective units less expensive.

Speed is probably one area where microprocessor based systems do not compare favorably with minicomputers. Most of the available microprocessors are based on MOS technology, and therefore operate at slower speeds than most common minicomputers based on TTL circuitry. Of course the fourth generation microprocessors, such as the Texas Instruments SBP0400, are beginning to approach the capabilities of minicomputers.

And finally microprocessors possess the unique advantage of ultracompact *size* which may be of significance in certain esoteric applications.

In addition to the technical criteria above, perhaps one of the most important business criteria for the selection of microprocessor system components should be mentioned: *availability*. The production of complex LSI components is an art as much as a science. A company that is expending considerable sums on system design and software development has to have assurances that the product is going to remain in production and available in reasonable quantities. One of the best ways is through second sourcing. Second sourcing refers to the licensing of another manufacturer to produce a given component. The new manufacturer then becomes a "second source" of that component, so that if the original manufacturer is no longer able to meet the supply of new orders, the second manufacturer would be able to handle them. The second sourcing of many of the more popular microprocessors has been a key factor in their widespread acceptance by OEMs with large-scale production requirements, as well as by contractors restricted from "sole-source" procurement.

MICROPROCESSOR SYSTEM FEASIBILITY

Once the appropriate system-design criteria have been established, it is the task of the system designer to determine the feasibility of implementing the system using microprocessors.

In determining whether a microprocessor implementation is feasible for a given application, three basic considerations must be carefully evaluated:

hardware structure
software structure
system integration

Hardware structure refers to the physical characteristics and specifications of the microprocessor chip itself: what are the voltages required, clock frequency and phase, power dissipation, packaging, and temperature and voltage operating ranges. Such considerations may not be significant for most applications, but high-reliability systems may impose constraints on the type of microprocessor that may be used in an application.

Software structure refers to the operational characteristics of the microprocessor: what is the number of registers, stacks, or buffers; what is the word length and addressing mode; what is the instruction set? What is the maximum memory size that can be directly addressed? Such questions are basic to any application, and the possibilities that the various microprocessors offer must be carefully investigated.

System integration is perhaps the most important consideration that must be studied. Microprocessors must be interfaced with ROM and RAM, with I/O devices, and with other system logic. Compatibility between components and systems must be maintained on both hardware (clocks, voltages) and software (word size, interrupts) levels. Such compatibility together with optimization of system resources are often difficult to achieve. For this reason, the leading microprocessor manufacturers have put together "kits" featuring almost everything from a chassis to a program debug aid. Since such kits are also less expensive than if one bought the individual components separately, there has been considerable interest in using such kits for system development work prior to finalization of the system design. A description of the use of these kits is presented in Chapter 7.

Another important factors in microprocessor selection is product life-cycle determination. Just like large-scale computers, microprocessors have gone through three "generations" of technology and design complexity. The threat of price/performance obsolescence is just as real with a microprocessor as with an IBM 1401 or 1620.

From a business or economic perspective, the question of product life-cycles and technological obsolescence is crucial to any system-design decision. For this reason, currently available microprocessors are not likely to appear in products with a long development lead-time. Such OEMs have opted for custom designed microprocessors to have greater control over product specifications and availability.

SELECTING THE MICROPROCESSOR

The task of selecting the microprocessor is the most crucial step in the system-design procedure. Once it has been determined that a microprocessor implementation is feasible for the intended application, the microprocessor should be selected on the basis of well established criteria. Since both hardware and software development depend on the particular microprocessor selected, microprocessor selection is one of the first steps in microcomputer system design.

In addition to such basic system design criteria as cost, flexibility, and compatibility, presented in the section above, certain additional criteria should also be applied to the selection of the microprocessor. These criteria include:

viability
second-source availability
systems and software support
upgrading potential

Viability is a novel yet very important concept in selecting a high technology product such as a microprocessor. Viability can simply be defined as being commercially producible on a relatively large scale. For a product as complex as a microprocessor, viability is not an immediately demonstrable concept. More than one microprocessor product has been designed and announced by a semiconductor manufacturer before it was realized that for various reasons it was not commercially producible. Some OEMs have already had the experience of being forced to terminate costly development projects because the prototype microprocessor which they were designed around never materialized into a viable product.

Second-source availability is another important criterion for selecting a microprocessor as it is for the microcomputer system components.

Systems and software support, such as microprocessor development systems, simulators, assemblers, software aids, and even training in programming and system design, are criteria particular to microprocessor selection that could be of essential importance to the OEM inexperienced in digital circuit logic design.

Finally, the upgrading potential of the microprocessor may be an important criteria for the user developing state-of-the-art equipment, such as military systems. As semiconductor technology progresses, the more popular microprocessors are being "upgraded" in terms of speed and operating environmental characteristics, thereby making them competitive with more recently announced microprocessors. Users of these products, therefore, are able to satisfy more demanding performance requirements without necessitating redesign around a newer microprocessor.

Once these commercial criteria have been considered, the system designer can evaluate the remaining contending microprocessors on technical criteria. One established method of comparing microprocessor performance is through the use of benchmark programs, which simulate the typical operations and calculations of the intended application. Through the use of benchmark testing, a comparison between microprocessors on the basis of two parameters may be made: the size of the program (in memory bytes), and the speed of execution of the program (in microseconds). Further information on benchmark testing in connection with microprocessor programming is presented in Chapter 6.

DESIGNING AUXILIARY HARDWARE

After the microprocessor has been selected, the auxiliary hardware necessary to make a system operative must also be selected and integrated into the system. Some microprocessor manufacturers have put together "kits" of compatible parts to simplify the task. Completely assembled prototype systems or "development systems" are also available and are discussed in greater detail in Chapter 7.

The basic auxiliary elements necessary to make the system operative are a power supply, a clock driver, a memory to supply a program, and an output circuit. Although such a minimal system would be suitable for a very limited application, most designs require considerably more capabilities and flexibility. Some of the additional elements that may be utilized in a microprocessor system design are:

flip-flops or latches
counters
decoders
interface circuits (TTL/MOS)

logic gates
A/D and D/A converters
communications interfaces

DEVELOPING SOFTWARE

The task of developing software comes after the analysis of the tradeoffs of hardware and software. Software is developed on the prototype system, or even on another computer using a cross assembler. There are advantages and disadvantages to each method of software development, but it is frequently more likely that more practical reasons, such as the availability of a prototype system or a cross assembler, determine which method of software development is actually used.

The time and expense required in developing software for a microprocessor system is one of the most frequently underestimated variables in microcomputer system design. The debugging, checkout, and testing phase of software development accounts for almost 50% of the total development effort. If one attempts to parametrize and quantify a software development effort in terms of the number of instructions per man-day, it will be determined that 5 to 15 instructions per man-day is a reasonable average. If the system designer is able to estimate the size of the program being developed, he should be able to make a reasonable estimate of the development resources required, as well as coordinate the software development with the hardware development.

INTEGRATING HARDWARE AND SOFTWARE

After the hardware and software has been designed, a prototype system can be constructed and the hardware and software integrated. At this point some of the more routine operational functions must be implemented: start-up, loading, error management. These functions require an interplay between hardware and software which must be carefully synchronized and controlled. For example, a hardware power-on detection circuit may initiate the loading or execution of a certain program. An interrupt in the form of an error or power failure must be detected and appropriate recovery measures initated.

New development systems feature emulators that permit emulation of various peripheral units before they are fully designed, permitting hardware and software to be developed simultaneously in a single unit. Such development systems are described in greater detail in Chapter 7.

DEBUGGING AND TESTING

The debugging and testing of a microprocessor system are crucial and difficult aspects of system design. It is often necessary to design special programs, simulators, or test considerations to analyze how the system will behave under a wide variety of occurrences.

One of the most important aspects of system design in this regard is to develop some technique, either in hardware or in software, to detect that something is wrong and to provide appropriate restarting and reloading procedures.

As certain microprocessors become widely used in the industry, commercial system analyzers are becoming available to make routine microprocessor function tests, and to monitor busses or registers, status and timing state variables on a single step basis for more detailed program and processor analysis and diagnosis. One example of such a System Analyzer is the Pro-Log M-821 for the Intel 8008, shown in Fig. 2.1.

DEVELOPING MAINTENANCE FACILITIES

Most microcomputer systems are designed for stand-alone use in the field or remote locations. Like any sophisticated electronic system it may from time to time require routine field maintenance. An important aspect of the reliability design of a microcomputer system is the provision of suitable maintenance facilities in the system.

There are a number of ways to implement maintenance facilities in a microcomputer system. Perhaps the easiest way is to provide a diagnostic program that will test the various operative units of the system, and provide an appropriate read-out or other indication of fault. Such a diagnostic program may be provided on a ROM which may be plugged into the system in the field in the place of the usual ROM for normal operation.

Another method of providing a maintenance facility is through error detection routines within the system control program itself. Various breakpoints could be established in a program, and the user would be able to diagnose the operation of the system on a real-time functional basis.

The provision of maintenance facilities for both hardware and software in a microcomputer system are important in the overall systems design.

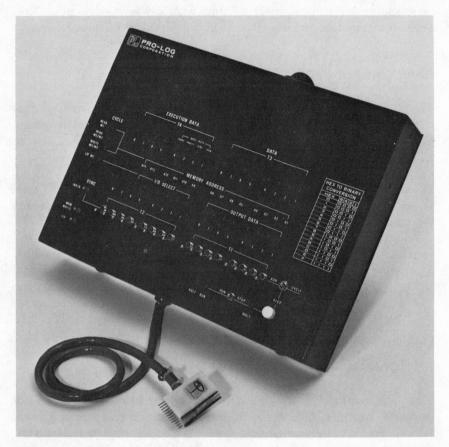

FIGURE 2.1 SYSTEM ANALYZER FOR INTEL 8008 SYSTEMS (PHOTOGRAPH COURTESY PRO-LOG CORPORATION).

MICROCOMPUTER ELEMENTS

Having described the task of the system designer in developing a microcomputer system, we can turn our attention to the basic microcomputer elements:

microprocessor
RAM
ROM
magnetic surface storage
I/O
interface components

Microprocessors

A microprocessor is the central processing unit (CPU) of a microcomputer on a single semiconductor "chip." The microprocessor performs the functions of sychronization and control, instruction decoding and execution, and handles I/O operations.

Microprocessors come in a wide variety of different technologies, architectures, capabilities, and associated supporting hardware and software. Such information for the available microprocessors is presented in Chapter 4. Here, however, we can list and define the various classifications and characteristics of microprocessors:

Technology. Microprocessors have been developed using almost all of the known semiconductor technologies: *p*-channel MOS (metal-oxide-semiconductor), *n*-channel MOS, complementary MOS, bipolar, and integrated-injection logic (I^2L). These and other technologies are treated in more detail in Chapter 3.

Architecture. Microprocessors are presently available in two basic architectural formats:

  a single-chip CPU
  a two-chip set, including one arithmetic and logic unit, and one microprogrammable control unit

The single-chip CPU is suitable for most applications where very high speed and instruction flexibility are not important considerations. The two-chip architecture features a control unit containing a read-only microprogram memory. The designer now has the flexibility to designate partticular arithmetic or logical functions as new machine instructions. Such functions are then stored in the microprogram memory and become machine microinstructions. Since such microinstructions are executed at a faster rate than regular machine instrutcions, the designer has effectively designed the microprocessor, through software, to execute his particular routines at optimum speed.

Microprocessors are generally classified by word organization and length. The first case is that of "slice" organization. In such organization the microprocessor has a word length that is a "slice" of the actual word length of the completed microcomputer system. For example, suppose the system designer needs a relatively long word length for his particular application, say 16 bits. To build such a system from slice architecture chips he merely connects the chips in parallel until a total of 16 bits is reached. If he is using a 2-bit slice unit (such as the Intel 3002), it would require eight such chips connected in parallel. The flexibility of such word organization is evident.

The second case of word organization is that of a stand-alone unit. The microprocessors are then classified by word length—4-bits, 8-bits, 12-bits, or 16-bits. The longer the word length, the more complex the chip and the more capabilities it has.

Architecture is also concerned with the internal features of the microprocessor. The number of registers, stacks, capabilities for interrupt, and direct-memory-access (DMA) are all important features in considering a microprocessor. Interface capabilities are also important from a systems viewpoint. Does the chip utilize a multiplexed bidirectional I/O bus, or have separate input and output lines, and separate address and data lines? Such considerations must be carefully examined by the system designer to determine what are the most important features required by his system, and which microprocessor includes such features.

Accessory Hardware. A microprocessor requires a clock driver and a voltage source to be operative. The clock driver is an externally packaged crystal-controlled oscillator that provides clock pulses with the appropriate phase to the microprocessor chip. In some cases the clock driver package is available as a member of the "parts family" available from the manufacturer of the microprocessor.

The voltage supply for the microprocessor is not supplied with the parts family and must be separately acquired by the user. The particular voltage requirements depend on the technology used in the microprocessor, as does the power dissipation.

The microprocessor requires a considerable amount of additional hardware to be fully operative as a microcomputer, including memory (RAM or ROM), I/O devices, and interface chips. In some systems up to 30 additional ICs must be provided to make a single microprocessor operative as a microcomputer.

Random-Access Memory

Memory is necessary in a microcomputer system to store programs and data used by the microprocessor. The amount of memory in a system depends on the application: the complexity of the program performing the processing operation, and the amount of data being handled by the processor.

Although the type of memory used by the microprocessor is not restricted, semiconductor memory is most commonly used. There are generally two types of memory chips available: RAM and ROM.

RAM refers to a memory store in which arbitrary binary data may be written into, and read from, the memory. ROM refers to a memory store from which predetermined binary information is readable from the memory.

RAM is used for loading new programs and new data into the processor, and for storing new results or new data as a result of the processing operation. ROM is used when a specific program or data will be used by the processor very frequently, thereby saving the necessity of loading the program or data into RAM every time the microcomputer is turned on. Since information is stored in a RAM in electrical form, if the power is turned off the contents of the RAM would not be preserved. On the other hand, in a ROM the information is physically written into the chip, so that if the power is turned off the content of the ROM is not affected.

Semiconductor RAM usually uses either bipolar or metal-oxide-semicondutor (MOS) technology.

Bipolar memories utilize standard bipolar transistors arranged as flip-flops in a basic storage cell as shown in Fig. 2.2. These storage cells are arranged in a cellular array as shown in Fig. 2.3, which forms the memory. Such memories are fabricated with or without on-chip decoding facilities. A decoder reduces the number of pins necessary on a chip, since the input signal need only specify the address of the memory location sought.

In addition to the multiple-emitter structure shown in Fig. 2.2, bipolar memories may also be fabricated using Schottky diodes, as shown in Fig.

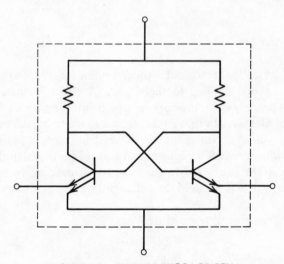

FIGURE 2.2 BIPOLAR STORAGE CELL.

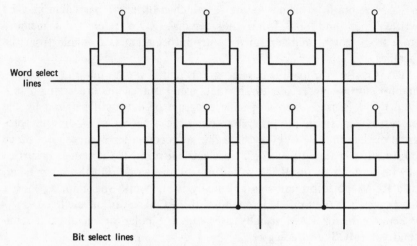

FIGURE 2.3   CELLULAR ARRAY.

2.4. Bipolar memories are typically available in 64-bit or 256-bit sizes.

MOS memories utilize arrangements of MOS field-effect transistors (MOSFETs) to store an addressable sequence of 1's and 0's. There are two types of MOS memory designs: static and dynamic. A static MOS memory (as shown in Fig. 2.5) is easier to drive and requires simplier external circuitry. The dynamic MOS memory (as shown in Fig. 2.6) requires clock signals to drive it but is generally less expensive than static memory design.

Read-Only Memory

A ROM is a device that reads out a predetermined stored code in response to an address signal applied to the device. A ROM is therefore distinguished from a read/write memory in which information cannot only be read from, but also written into a predetermined memory address.

ROMs are typically used to supply dot matrix patterns for use in character generation on a CRT alpha-numeric display. In microprogrammed computers, a ROM is utilized to store microinstructions. In a microprocessor system, a ROM is used to store programs for execution by the system.

There are three general types of ROMs:

masked
field programmable (fusible link)
erasable (floating gate)

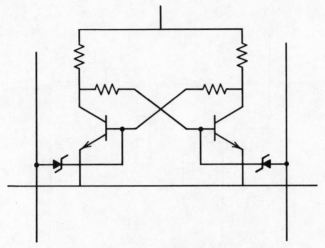

FIGURE 2.4   SCHOTTKY DIODE MEMORY.

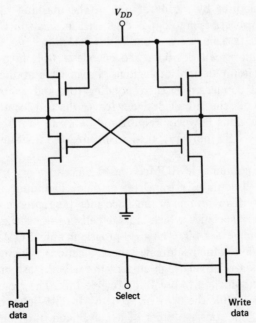

FIGURE 2.5   STATIC MOS MEMORY.

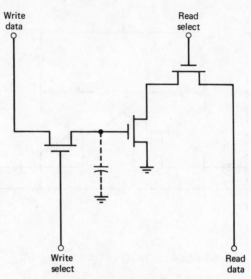

FIGURE 2.6   DYNAMIC MOS MEMORY.

The masked ROM is particularly suited for high-volume applications. The memory bit pattern is produced during actual fabrication of the chip by the manufacturer by means of one of the masking operations (integrated circuit process technology is discussed in detail in Chapter 3). The memory matrix is defined by X and Y bit selection lines which form the individual memory cell positions. To encode a 1-bit in a particular cell position, the circuit design implements a transistor at that cell location, with electrodes connected to corresponding row and column select lines. To encode a 0-bit, the circuit designer leaves the cell location empty.

Many applications however require only a small number of ROMs. In these situations it is more practical to utiliize the field-programmable or erasable ROMs.

The field-programmable ROM is based on a memory matrix in which each storage cell contains a transistor or diode including a fuse (or "fusible link") in series with one of the electrodes (as represented in Fig. 2.7). The programmer specifies which storage cell positions (i.e., address locations) should have a 1-bit. The field-programmable ROM is placed in a programming unit which addresses those locations which should have a 1-bit and sends a relatively high current through the associated transistor, diode, and fuse sufficient to break the fusible link. The closed fusible links represent 0 bits, while the open or "blown" fusible links represent 1 bits.

The fusible link consists either of a polysilicon, nichrome, or titanium tungsten strip which is deposited between the electrodes of the internal

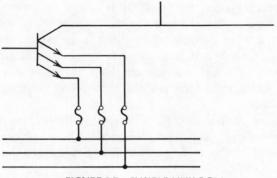

FIGURE 2.7   FUSIBLE LINK ROM.

transistors and the row and column sense lines. When an excessive current is applied along the strip, the link breaks, as shown in Fig. 2.8.

One disadvantage of the fusible-link ROM is that its programming is
permanent. Once the fusible links have been blown, the bit pattern programmed into the ROM cannot be changed. Although this may not be
important if the ROM is expected to be used a substantial number of
times, it is clearly not practical to use a fusible-link ROM if the designer
is merely testing out a ROM program which may only be used a relatively
small number of times before being discarded. The device designed for
such requirements is the erasable ROM.

Another disadvantage of the fusible link ROM is that occasionally a
"blown" link may, over a period of time, "regrow" and close, becoming
a closed link. Such occurrences are not common and are the result of in-
completely broken links.

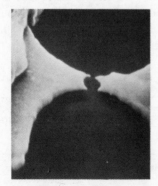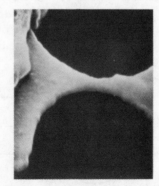

FIGURE 2.8   A "BLOWN" FUSIBLE LINK (*LEFT*), COMPARED WITH ORIGINAL LINK
(*RIGHT*).

Another type of programmable ROM is based on avalanche-induced migration technology. A fused junction can be formed in such a device by providing a relatively high current through the emitter-base-collector region. The region of current flow contracts into a narrow channel which consequently reaches a high temperature. Metallization which is adjacent to this region melts and shorts out the base-emitter junction, leaving a base-collector diode.

The erasable or floating-gate ROM is electrically programmable, erasable by ultraviolet light, and reprogrammable. The erasibility feature of the ROM is based on the floating silicon gate structure of the chip itself, shown in Fig. 2.9.

The structure shown in Fig. 2.9 is that of a p-channel MOSFET. (A more detailed description of MOS technology is presented in Chapter 3.) A silicon gate is situated within the silicon dioxide layer, and normally effectively isolates the source from the drain electrodes.

During programming, a relatively high negative voltage is applied to the p-n junction of a predetermined memory cell. This large reverse voltage results in the phenomenon of *junction breakdown*. The free electrons and holes have such high kinetic energy that some of the silicon-silicon bonds become torn apart, thereby resulting in additional charge carriers being formed. This avalanche process results in the injection of electrons into the floating silicon gate.

After the applied voltage is removed the silicon gate retains its negative charge, since it is electrically isolated and has no ground or discharge path.

The presence of the electrically charged silicon gate directly above the n-type silicon substrate results in the formation of a conductive inversion region in the substrate. Since the silicon gate extends between the doped regions beneath the source and the drain, the net result is that a conductive layer is formed in the substrate extending between the source and the drain. The presence or absence of this conductive layer is a particular memory cell position determines the binary 1 bit or 0 bit stored in that cell.

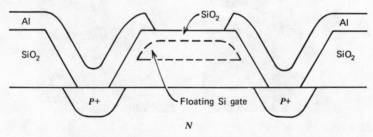

FIGURE 2.9   FLOATING SILICON GATE STRUCTURE.

Erasure of the memory takes place by illuminating the surface of the chip with ultraviolet light. A transparent lid or window is provided in the sealed package over the chip so that the user may perform the erasing operation after the chip has been packaged and programmed in the field.

Magnetic Surface Storage

One of the most common techniques of off-line storage in a microcomputer system is magnetic surface storage. Magnetic surface storage is achieved by recording sequential patterns of magnetization on a "track" of a magnetic storage medium, typically a magnetic film or layer. The magnetic film may be provided on a wide variety of storage mediums, including webs of tape, a cartridge or cassette, disk pack or diskette, drum, card strip, or similar configurations.

Data bits are represented on a track by a sequence of regions of magnetization or nonmagnetization. These are several methods of representing these data, depending on the particular coding technique, including Non-Return-to-Zero (NRZ), Return-to-Zero (RZ), Miller Code, and Manchester Code.

The NRZ method (Fig. 2.10a) is the straightforward technique of representing 0 bit by a zero-level signal, and a 1 bit by a one-level pulse.

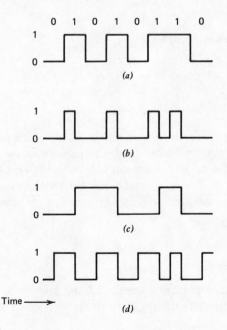

FIGURE 2.10 DATA RECORDING METHODS. (A) NRZ; (B) RZ; (C) MILLER; (D) MANCHESTER (PHASE ENCODING).

The RZ method (Fig. 2.10b) is based on a different clocking technique. Although a 0 bit is represented by a zero-level signal, a 1-bit is represented by a pulse that rises to the one level and then "returns to zero" within one cycle or bit time.

Miller Code represents a 1-bit by a pulse transition in the middle of the cycle; a 0-bit is represented by no transition during the cycle, followed by a transition to the one level at the end of the cycle. If the level is already at the one level, no transition at the end of the cycle is made, as shown in Fig. 2.10c.

Manchester Code (or phase encoding) utilizes a transition in the middle of each cycle to represent either a 0-bit or a 1-bit. A 1-bit is represented by a transition from the one level to the zero level, while a 0-bit is represented by a transition from the zero level to the one level.

I/O

The microcomputer system can operate with a wide variety of input and output devices. Some of the standard input devices include:

  keyboard (solid state or Teletype)
  tape readers (paper or magnetic)
  card readers (paper or magnetic)
  disk drives (standard and floppy)
  optical readers (mark and character)

Some of the standard output devices include:

  punches (card and paper tape)
  printers (impact and nonimpact)
  displays
  plotters

It is the problem of the system designer to determine which of these devices is most suitable for the given application and interface the device to the microcomputer. Such interfacing is done through interfacing chips and utilizing special hardware or software to make the external device compatible with the logic levels, timing, and synchronization of the processor.

Interface Logic

Interface logic is one of the most important elements of the microcomputer system. A microprocessor operates on its own clocks and has its own internal characteristics that cannot be modified by the user. External devices, such as I/O devices, transducers, and the like also have their own characteristics. To make the processor able to control and process data associated with such external devices, it is necessary to properly code and synchronize the elements of the system. At the first level this is done through hardware—utilizing appropriate latches, decoders or encoders, or converters to make the signals from one system element usable by another system element. Once such basic physical and electrical compatibility between the diverse elements of the system is achieved, a second and more sophisticated level of system integration may be implemented. This second level of integration may be achieved in software, rather than in hardware. For example, suppose an external device uses ASCII code. An ASCII-to-binary code conversion may be made through software, once the simple electrical connections are made in the system between the external device and the microprocessor.

The microprocessor manufacturers have recognized that such interface logic is absolutely necessary for implementing a microprocessor system. Accordingly, as a convenience to the system designer, these manufacturers have assembled "parts families" of the most frequently used IC components for sale with the microprocessor. Such parts families are usually priced below the separate total cost of the components, so that it is economically advantageous for the designer to purchase such parts from the microprocessor manufacturer. Some simple microprocessor systems that can be constructed with the parts family of the Intel 4040 microprocessor are presented in a later chapter.

If the microcomputer system is to be utilized in conjunction with remote devices, some type of communications interface device must be provided. These communications interface devices perform the functions of parallel-to-serial or serial-to-parallel conversion, synchronization, and transmission control.

The basic function of the communications interface device is to convert the bit-parallel data stream coming from the processor or memory into a serial data stream for transmission along a data channel or communications link. At the other end of the transmission system, the serial data stream must in turn be converted into a bit-parallel data stream for use by the other processor or terminal.

These communications interface functions have been implemented on a LSI chip, which is referred to as a UART or ACIA. The basic structural elements of the UART and ACIA are illustrated in Fig. 2.11.

The UART is a universal asynchronous receiver/transmitter. The ACIA is an asynchronous communication interface adapter. Both of these LSI devices utilize clocked shift registers to transfer parallel information to

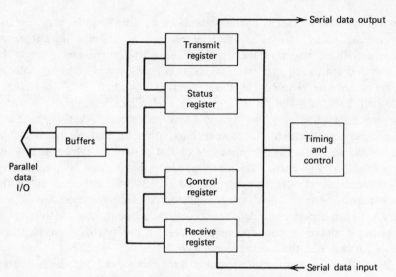

FIGURE 2.11   UART OR ACIA.

serial format and vice versa. Transmission control bits, such as a start and stop bit, as well as a parity bit, are also automatically added to the serial data stream.

CHAPTER THREE
TECHNOLOGY OF
MICROPROCESSORS

As we pointed out in Chapter 1, the development of microprocessors has been made possible by advances in semiconductor process technology. To give a better appreciation of the various process and circuit technologies employed in the fabrication of microprocessors, we review in this chapter these technologies with particular attention to their application in microprocessor design and fabrication.

Before we present the technical details of these technologies, it is appropriate to place the development of microprocessors in historical perspective, beginning with the integrated circuit.

INTEGRATED CIRCUIT (IC) TECHNOLOGY

One of the most important developments in semiconductor technology was that of the IC in the early 1960s. As opposed to discrete components, an IC comprises a number of electronic circuit components which are fabricated and packaged as a single unit. Two key technological developments made IC technology possible: the development of the planar silicon crystal wafer and the development of thin-film technology.

Before the development of the planar silicon wafer, semiconductor components were fabricated using the grown junction or the alloy junction method. Although such fabrication techniques were suitable for discrete components, they are impractical for larger scale integrated circuits. A planar silicon crystal wafer, on the other hand, permits active components to be defined thereon separated by an insulating oxide layer or region.

Planar silicon crystal wafers are formed by slicing them from a substantially cylindrical ingot of crystalline silicon. The wafers are typically 2 to 3 in. in diameter and 16 to 20 mils thick.

Thin-film technology then enables one to define active components or insulating regions on the wafer by means of a photolithographic process. The photolithographic process begins by defining individual circuits on a *composite* drawing (Fig. 3.1). The composite defines the various regions

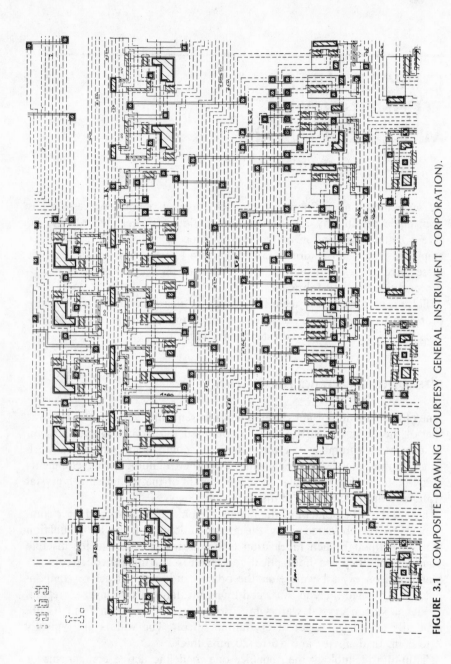

FIGURE 3.1 COMPOSITE DRAWING (COURTESY GENERAL INSTRUMENT CORPORATION).

and layers of the circuit in terms of the various processing steps, as presented in a two-dimensional representation (Fig. 3.2).

To physically define the various regions and layers of the circuit on the silicon wafer, several photographic *masks* are utilized. Each mask corresponds to a single processing step of the wafer. The various required masks are produced from the composite, then photographically reduced in size to the actual size of the IC. A step-and-repeat camera repeats the mask image both vertically and horizontally over a final mask or working plate.

The circuits are defined on the wafer first by applying a photosensitive layer over the wafer. One of the masks is then placed over the layer and exposed to light. The pattern of the mask has therefore been transferred to the wafer. To imbed this pattern within the wafer itself, an etching solution is applied to the surface of the wafer which selectively penetrates those areas which have been exposed. This photolithographic process is

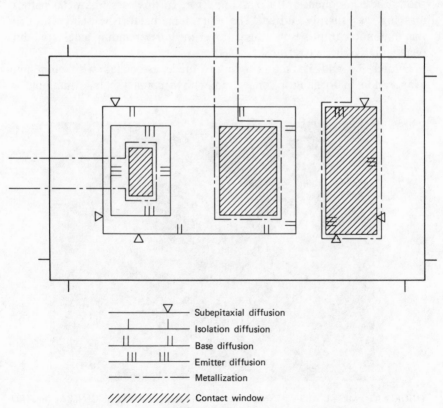

FIGURE 3.2 CIRCUIT REPRESENTATION ON COMPOSITE DRAWING.

repeated a number of times with the different masks until the final circuit is defined on the wafer. The number of type of processing steps are different for different circuit types and technologies, which are defined in more detail in the following sections.

Wafer fabrication by means of a photolithographic process is the most critical aspect of IC production. The accuracy of each of the masking and processing steps affects the operability and reliability of the final component. In large-scale ICs, with thousands of components on a single chip, it is the semiconductor process technology that determines whether a particularly complex chip can be commercially fabricated. More than one microprocessor product has been announced by a manufacturer before it was realized that it wash not commercially producible. Even one major user designed and developed a product around such a microprocessor that was never successfully produced.

In this connection, it is worthwhile to illustrate some typical processing errors that may result in device failure or decreased reliability. Figure 3.3 shows the consequence of a masking error. In this case the metal pattern masking was slightly shifted. The aluminum metal (the shiny strips in the photomicrograph) is misaligned over the corresponding gates (the dull rectangularly shaped regions).

Figures 3.4 and 3.5 shows a failure mode associated with aluminum evaporation in forming a connection with a contact hole. Aluminum is

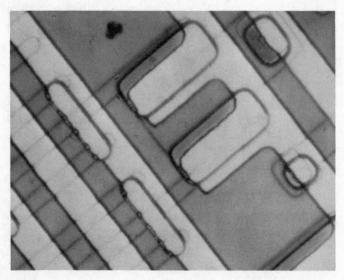

FIGURE 3.3 METAL MISALIGNMENT OVER GATES (COURTESY GENERAL INSTRUMENT CORP.).

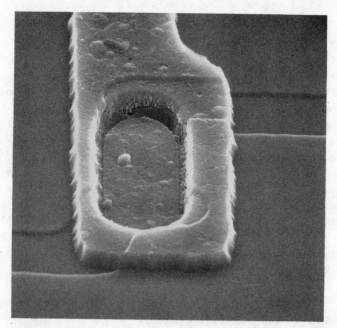

FIGURE 3.4 CONTACT HOLE WITH A POSSIBLE EDGE FAULT (COURTESY GENERAL INSTRUMENT CORP.).

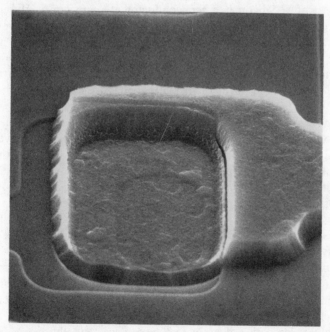

FIGURE 3.5 CONTACT HOLE WITH A POSSIBLE EDGE FAULT (COURTESY GENERAL INSTRUMENT CORP.).

applied to the wafer by means of electron beam evaporation. In the case
of a contact hole, electrical connection between the two different layers
on the wafer is achieved by the evaporated aluminum on the nearly vertical contact wall. The thickness of the aluminum on the wall is not uniform, and tiny microcracks, such as in the rear edge of the wall shown in
Fig. 3.4, or the right edge of that in Fig. 3.5, may result. The consequence
of such a fault is decreased reliability; although an electrical connection
is made between the layers, the interconnection is a very narrow one, and
the heat generated by the high current density along the connection path
may lead to the connection failure.

Figures 3.4 and 3.5 are scanning electron microscope (SEM) photo-
graphs at a magnification of 3000X. The use of the SEM, which permits
a perspective view of the components and surface of the chips, is very
useful in examining and analyzing such failure modes.

PLANAR SILICON PROCESS TECHNOLOGY

A description of the planar silicon process is fundamental in understanding
IC technology. As noted above, the process begins with the production of
a silicon wafer. Silicon is a semiconductor at room temperature and has
an energy gap (1.1 eV) which is particularly useful for electronic components over a wide temperature range. More importantly, the major advantage of silicon as a substrate for an IC is the simplicity of creating an
insulating layer or region on the wafer. By exposing the wafer to air under
suitable conditions, a layer of insulating silicon dioxide is formed on the
wafer.

A component or circuit is formed on the substrate by a pattern of active
and insulating regions. Electronic circuits operate by the movement of
charge from one circuit element to another. Because of its crystal structure, pure silicon is not practical for this purpose. However, by incorporating impurity atoms into the crystal structure, replacing silicon atoms,
it is possible to change the conductivity characteristics of the crystal lattice. By replacing a silicon atom in the crystal lattice with an atom with
a different valence, such as phosphorus or boron, one can affect the conductivity of the wafer.

Phosphorus, for example, has five valence electrons, compared with
silicon's four valence electrons. When an impurity atom of phosphorus is
incorporated in the silicon crystal lattice (Fig. 3.6), an extra electron having a relatively small ionization energy is added to the lattice. At room
temperature, ionization does in fact take place, and the extra electron is
freed to transport charge from one region of the substrate to another.

In the case of a phosphorus dopant, the charge carriers are negative

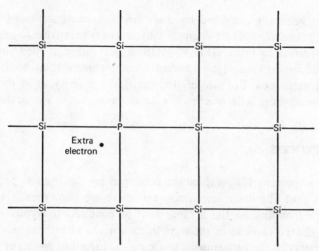

FIGURE 3.6 SILICON LATTICE WITH DOPANT IMPURITY.

(i.e., electrons), and therefore the doped silicon is referred to as *n*-type silicon. In the case of a boron dopant, there is an electron deficiency (i.e., a hole), and the charge carriers in boron doped silicon are positive (i.e., holes), and so the doped silicon is called *p*-type.

The sequence of planar silicon processing steps can now be described. High purity silicon is first zone refined to remove trace impurities. The pure silicon is remelted in a crucible. A seed crystal is then introduced into the melt, which has been doped with the appropriate type and concentration of impurities. The silicon melt then rearranges itself in the same lattice configuration as the seed crystal and solidifies in that configuration as it cools. This process, known as crystal pulling, results in the substantially cylinderical ingot of doped crystalline silicon.

After slicing, lapping, and polishing the wafers from the silicon ingot, the photolitographic process of defining and interconnecting individual components on the wafer begins.

There are two basic types of electronic components that may be fabricated with IC technology, and correspondingly two basic types of processes. These two basic component types are *bipolar* and *unipolar*. These designations refer to the type of charge carrier present in the device. In a bipolar device, there are two charge carriers of opposite polarity; in a unipolar device there is only one charge carrier. The most important type of unipolar device that is fabricated with IC technology is the planar metal-insulator-semiconductor (MIS) structure, more commonly known as MOS.

Within each of the broad categories of bipolar and unipolar (MOS) there are a number of distinct configurations and processing techniques. Bipolar devices are generally classified by their circuit type: transistor-transistor-logic (T²L), emitter-coupled-logic (ECL), resistor-transistor logic (RTL), and diode-transistor logic (DTL). MOS devices are classified initally on the basis of conductivity type (*p*-channel or *n*-channel), as well as other processing variations. Because of the significant differences in these processing technologies, it is worthwhile to examine them in greater detail.

BIPOLAR PROCESS

The most important IC components produced by the bipolar process are transistors. Just like discrete components, there are two types of transistor structures depending on the arrangement of conductivity types: *npn* and *pnp*. The charge carriers in the *npn* transistor are electrons; whereas the charge carriers in the *pnp* transistor are holes. Electrons have substantially greater mobility than holes, and thus the electrical characteristics of the *npn* transistor provide faster response time (frequency response) and gain. Such electrical characteristics are directly proportional to the "transport factor" of the charge carriers in the transistor base. Since the *npn* transistor is most commonly used in integrated circuits, the structure and fabrication of the *npn* type are particularly noted here.

The composite representation and cross section of a typical *npn* transistor are shown in Fig. 3.7. Some of the more important structural features of the npn transistor are shown in the cross sectional view, including the base (B), emitter (E), and collector (C) contacts; isolation regions, isolating the transistor from other circuit components; and a buried layer, for providing a more conductive path between the collector and the base and emitter.

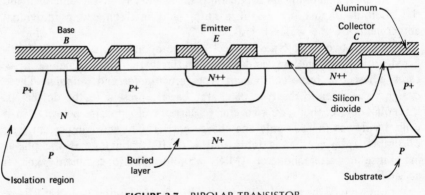

FIGURE 3.7   BIPOLAR TRANSISTOR.

Schottky Bipolar

The selection of an appropriate logic family for implementing a bipolar technology depends to a great extent on the semiconductor process technology considerations. The ability to create a diode, called a Schottky diode, by means of a simple process step makes a DTL implementation particularly advantageous, and even competitive with T²L or ECL bipolar implementations.

The basic structure of the Schottky transistor is shown in Fig. 3.8. This figure should be carefully compared with Fig. 3.7. It is seen that the aluminum base structure extends beyond the P+ doped region. Thus another electronic component is formed from the single base electrode, an aluminum-silicon junction diode parallel to the base-collector circuit of the transistor.

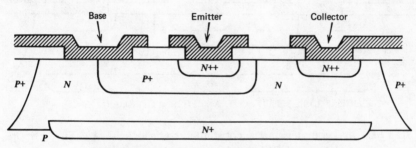

FIGURE 3.8   SCHOTTKY BIPOLAR TRANSISTOR.

Discrete Schottky diodes, also known as surface-barrier diodes, have been well known for years as low-noise components and are represented by the schematic symbol shown in Fig. 3.9a. The symbol representing the Schottky transistor is based on this representation and is shown in Fig. 3.9b.

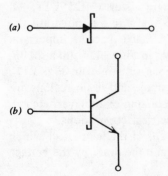

(a)

(b)

FIGURE 3.9   (A) SCHOTTKY DIODE SCHEMATIC; (B) SCHOTTKY TRANSISTOR SCHEMATIC.

In practice, the structure of the Schottky transistor shown in Fig. 3.8 does not have good reproducibility in production size runs. Instead, a structure incorporating guard rings as shown in Fig. 3.10 is utilized. The guard ring isolates the Schottky diode from the edge of the silicon dioxide layer, which led to the highly undesirable variable characteristics in each device.

Other Bipolar Technologies

In addition to the technologies noted above, a number of other bipolar technologies are in the developmental stages and should be noted here for completeness. These include triple-diffused emitter-follower logic

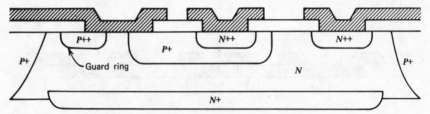

FIGURE 3.10   SCHOTTKY TRANSISTOR WITH GUARD RINGS.

(3D EFL), and complementary constant-current logic (C³L). Furthermore, emitter-coupled logic (ECL) is also relevant for microprocessor applications, and at least one microprocessor using that technology has already been announced.

MOS PROCESS

The MOS process refers to the fabrication of an MOS device. The most important such device is the MOS field-effect transistor (MOSFET). Although the FET has been known for over 20 years, it was not until the MOS process was commercialized in the 1960s that it became important.

The basic structure of the MOSFET is shown in Fig. 3.11a. Like the bipolar device, it is formed on a p or n-type silicon substrate. In Fig. 3.11a an n-type silicon substrate is shown. Discrete source and drain regions are diffused into the substrate, covered with an insulating oxide layer, etched, and then finally metallized to produce the electrical connections.

As the name implies, a FET operates by means of the field effect which is produced in the channel between the source and the drain by the voltage on the gate.

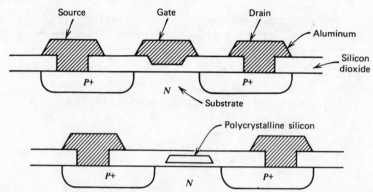

FIGURE 3.11 (A) MOS FIELD EFFECT TRANSISTOR; (B) SILICON GATE MOS TRANSISTOR.

Another important MOS transistor configuration is the *silicon gate* MOS device, shown in cross-sectional view in Fig. 3.11b. The silicon gate device includes a polycrystalline silicon region within the oxide layer replacing the aluminum gate. The silicon gate MOS device has three basic advantages:

conductance is possible at lower gate threshold voltage
greater densities are possible
the lower internal parasitic capacitance results in greater device speeds

One disadvantage of the silicon gate process is that it is a more complex fabrication procedure, requiring several more masking steps than a metal gate process.

Ion implanted MOS devices should also be considered. An ion implanted device is produced by the process of accurately directing dopant ions into specific portions of the silicon wafer surface, thereby "implanting" them. The purpose of ion implantation is to achieve greater control over the magnitude of the threshold voltage.

A cross-sectional view of a typical ion-implanted MOS device is shown in Fig. 3.12, with the ion implantation being directed in the channel region

MOS devices may be fabricated in two basic characteristic types: depletion mode and enhancement mode. These two types refer to the conductivity of the device with respect to the applied gate voltage. In an enhancement type device, current flow is blocked between the source and the drain unless a voltage is applied to the gate. In a depletion type device current is able to flow between the source and the drain without any gate voltage applied. The current cut-off in a depletion mode device occurs at a higher voltage called the threshold voltage. The standard schematic symbols for *n*-channel and *p*-channel MOSFETS of depletion and enhancement mode types are shown in Fig. 3.13.

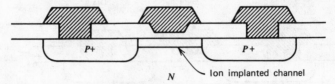

FIGURE 3.12   ION IMPLANTED MOS TRANSISTOR.

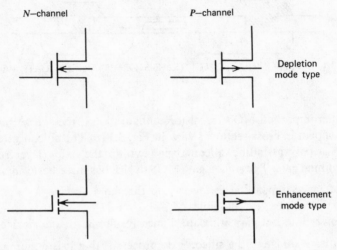

FIGURE 3.13   MOS TRANSISTOR SCHEMATIC.

In practice, the source electrode is often connected internally to the substrate, and the simplified schematic symbols for n-channel and p-channel MOS devices in Fig. 3.14 are frequently used.

Typical circuit configurations of enhancement and depletion mode MOS devices are shown in Fig. 3.15. Also shown with these circuit configurations are the corresponding current versus voltage characteristic curves. The characteristic curve associated with the depletion mode device indicates a relatively constant current until the point $V_0 = V_{DD} - V_T$, as opposed to the rapidly decaying current level associated with the enhancement mode circuit. Depletion mode devices thus allow a faster charging time than enhancement mode devices.

Complementary-Symmetry MOS (C-MOS)

C-MOS devices utilize both p-channel and n-channel MOS devices on a single chip. As shown in Fig. 3.16, a cross-sectional view of an n-channel

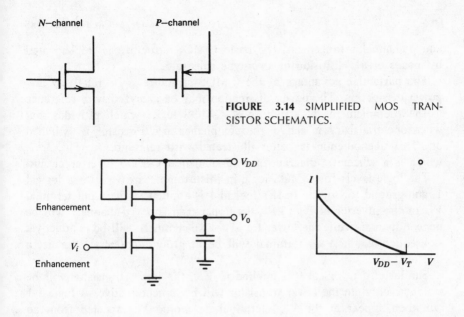

N–channel   P–channel

FIGURE 3.14 SIMPLIFIED MOS TRANSISTOR SCHEMATICS.

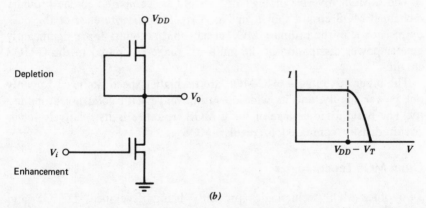

V_{DD}

Enhancement

V_0

V_i

Enhancement

I

$V_{DD} - V_T$ V

V_{DD}

Depletion

V_0

V_i

Enhancement

I

$V_{DD} - V_T$ V

(b)

FIGURE 3.15 TYPICAL MOS CIRCUIT CONFIGURATIONS AND CHARACTERISTIC CURVES.

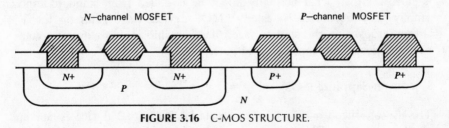

N–channel MOSFET   P–channel MOSFET

N+   N+   P+   P+

P

N

FIGURE 3.16 C-MOS STRUCTURE.

and p-channel arrangement, the basic C-MOS structure is implemented by means of a p-diffusion in an n-type substrate.

The particular advantage of the C-MOS structure is its relatively low power dissipation. The power dissipation may be analyzed with reference to the "complementary" structure of C-MOS logic, which provides that when one transistor is active, the complementary transistor is switched off. This phenomenon is better illustrated with references to Fig. 3.17, which is a schematic diagram of a fundamental C-MOS inverter circuit.

The logic levels for C-MOS logic in this example are V_{DD} for a logical 1, and ground for logical 0. If a logical 1 is applied to the input terminal V_{IN} of the inverter of Fig. 3.17, the upper transistor (p-channel) will be nonconductive, while the lower transistor (n-channel) will be conductive. Consequently, the V_{OUT} terminal will be at ground potential, that is, a logical 0.

Similarly, if a logical 0 is applied to V_{IN}, the upper transistor will be conductive, while the lower transistor will be nonconductive. A logical 1 will then appear at the V_{OUT} terminal, as would be expected from an inverter.

The C-MOS inverter of Fig. 3.17 should be compared to the ordinary n-channel MOS circuit shown in Fig. 3.18. It is the presence of the pull-up resistor R in the ordinary MOS circuit that accounts for a significantly greater power dissipation in the milliwatt range compared to the C-MOS circuit.

The other advantages of C-MOS are its higher speed, its need for only one power supply, and its wide operating range with good noise immunity. The basic disadvantage of the C-MOS structure is its relatively lower circuit density compared to regular MOS.

Other MOS Technologies

Two other MOS technologies presently being developed, D-MOS and V-MOS, should also be noted. D-MOS is a technique of using double diffusion (i.e. two successive diffusions) through the same silicon oxide window. As a result, the channel between the source and drain diffusions is narrower than what normally might be obtained from standard lithography, and the device is faster. V-MOS devices have gates on the V-shaped grooves on the chip surface, thereby achieving an extremely compact and dense implementation of gates.

Silicon-on-Sapphire (SOS)

The use of silicon as the substrate material for an IC device is not an absolute necessity. The active regions of silicon which are used for form-

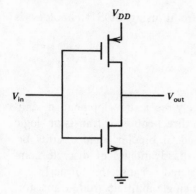

FIGURE 3.17 C-MOS INVERTER CIRCUIT.

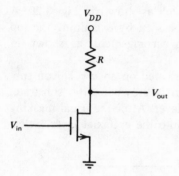

FIGURE 3.18 MOS INVERTER CIRCUIT.

ing portions of an electronic component may be placed on a substrate of any material which has substantially similar physical properties as silicon. The key physical property, due to the criticalness of the relative placement of the silicon regions in determining their electrical characteristics, is the coefficient of thermal expansion. The substance with a coefficient of thermal expansion relatively close to that of silicon, and therefore widely used for such applications is sapphire. The resulting technology is called silicon-on-sapphire (SOS), and its most important applications have been in the area of C-MOS circuits.

Sapphire is an insulator, permitting the active silicon regions for the various components to be deposited directly on the surface of the sapphire substrate, separated only by distance and an oxide layer. Guard rings, which are normally necessary for C-MOS implementations, are unnecessary, thereby increasing the density of the circuits on a given chip area. Another important feature of an SOS implementation is the elimination of parasitic capacitances which are present between the electrodes and the substrate of ordinary MOS devices. Such capacitances result in decreased speed and greater power consumption.

A cross-sectional view of a C-MOS circuit using SOS technology is shown in Fig. 3.19.

Integrated Injection Logic (I^2L)

Integrated injection logic (I^2L) is a relatively recent development in semi-conductor process technology based on direct-coupled transistor logic (DCTL). DCTL has not been widely used in bipolar logic circuits because of its relatively poor stability. The disadvantages of discrete component DCTL have been essentially eliminated because the formerly discrete components are now integrated into a single multielectrode transistor.

The basic building block of an I^2L circuit is a multielectrode *n-p-n* transistor coupled with a *p-n-p* transistor, such as shown in Fig. 3.20. A better conception of the I^2L structure can be seen by examining the top view and cross section of typical transistor arrangement, as shown in Fig. 3.21.

The I^2L device shown in Fig. 3.21 is fabricated on an $n+$ silicon substrate. An epitaxial layer of *n*-type material is grown on the substrate, thereby defining the $n+$ region as a buried layer. After the usual masking operations, two *p*-type diffusions are made into the epitaxial layer. Selec-

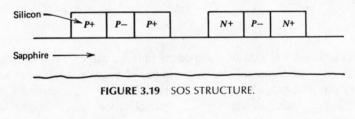

FIGURE 3.19   SOS STRUCTURE.

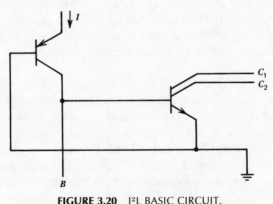

FIGURE 3.20 I^2L BASIC CIRCUIT.

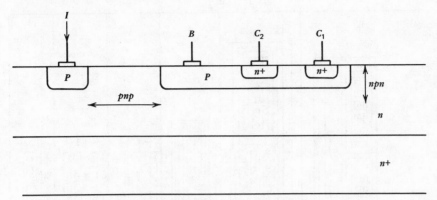

FIGURE 3.21 I²L STRUCTURE.

tive $n+$ type diffusions are then made to define both lateral and vertical transistors.

The resulting I²L circuit offers important improvements in speed, power dissipation, density, and process technology over most other circuit technologies. As can be seen from the relatively simple structure of the device shown in Fig. 3.21, the process technology is relatively easy. The greater packing density of I²L technology is graphically portrayed in Fig. 3.22, compared with similar process technologies. Finally, the speed and power of the I²L circuit compares favorably with the other technologies, as illustrated in the last section.

MICROPROCESSSOR TECHNOLOGY

Just like large-scale computer systems, microprocessors have gone through four "generations." Although the specification of what characteristics constitute a "generation" is a matter of choice, there are some definitive milestones in the development of microprocessor technology that merit the designation of a "generation."

With such qualifications in mind, we suggest that the "first generation" of microprocessors, typified by the Intel 4004, were "calculator" type chips with a limited instruction set and based on p-channel MOS technology. The "second generation," typified by the Intel 8080, were characterized by a larger instruction set (up to 80 instructions), and n-channel MOS technology. The "third generation," typified by the Intel 3001/2, utilized more sophisticated architecture and bipolar technology. Finally, the characteristics of the "fourth generation" are now just emerging. Texas Instruments SBP 0400 is one such processor that could be considered

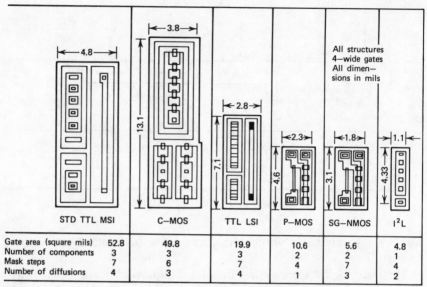

FIGURE 3.22 LAYOUT COMPARISONS (REPRINTED BY PERMISSION FROM *ELEC-TRONICS*, FEB. 6, 1975; COPYRIGHT © McGRAW-HILL, INC. 1975).

"fourth generation," featuring a highly sophisticated programmable logic array microprogramming structure, and integrated injection logic (I^2L) technology.

The rapid growth in both bipolar and MOS technology may be represented by the increase in the number of gates per chip, and the memory size per chip, between the years 1970 and 1975. The price changes on a per gate or per memory bit scale are also worth noting, as shown in Table 3.1.

Microprocessors, like any other bipolar or MOS component, have gone through similar drops in prices. As noted in Chapter 2, one of the important factors in determining microprocessor system feasibility is the problem of technological obsolescence or price/performance erosion. Before analyzing the problem of technological obsolescence in a later section, we must consider the various factors which affect the cost of microprocessor design and fabrication.

The important factors that are considered in the design of a microprocessor chip are:

the size of the chip
the clock rate and other physical requirements
the number of gates
the number of processing steps, that is, the technology

TABLE 3.1

Gates per chip		
Technology	1970	1975
Bipolar	150	1000
MOS	1000	5000

Memory size per chip (bits of random access memory)		
Technology	1970	1975
Bipolar	256	1024
MOS	1024	4096

Price per gate (cents)		
	1970	1975
Bipolar	10	3
MOS	1	0.3

Price per bit of memory (cents)		
	1970	1975
Bipolar	6	0.6–1.0
MOS	2	0.3–0.5

Each of these factors have an important effect on the cost of producing the microprocessor chip and ultimately on the price of the microprocessor to the user. A better indication of the components of the microprocessor fabrication cost may be shown in the following breakdown:

wafer	$5 per wafer
wafer fabrication	$75
wafer testing	$10
assembly	$0.60 per circuit
final test	$0.10 per circuit

Although these figures are rough estimates that may vary from process to process and manufacturer to manufacturer, they illustrate that the major component of microprocessor fabrication cost is in testing.

The first test is the wafer test. One or more test transistors are incorporated at one or two test locations on the wafer. These test transistors have a slightly larger dimension than the regular transistors in the IC to facility external probing and testing. The wafer is placed in a testing facility and probes separated by a distance of about 4 mils (100 microns) test the operation of the transistors. If the test transistors are inoperative, for example, due to poor mask alignment, the wafer is discarded.

The acceptable wafers are then placed in an automatic wafer probe tester, where a preliminary test of each chip on the wafer is made. Chips that fail this preliminary test are automatically marked with an ink dot for visually indicating the defective circuits. The following physical fabrication steps then take place:

scribing the wafer
breaking the wafer into individual chips ("dicing")
visually die sorting the defective ones
bonding the chip to a package
bonding the leads to the pads on the chip
sealing the package
testing

In addition to merely operational testing, quantitative tests are also made to verify the gain and other operating characteristics of the device. Such tests measure the structural integrity of the various layers and isolation regions, and therefore check the reliability of the device.

In addition to the fabrication cost, consideration must also be given to the cost of designing and developing the microprocessor. Estimates vary here, but the following rough figures may be presented to indicate the time required for a small design group experienced in digital logic technology to develop a microprocessor:

architecture and instruction set: 1 to 2 months
circuit design and testing: 1 to 2 months
software development: 2 to 3 months
LSI process technology: 2 to 3 months
total development time: 6 to 10 months

The actual cost depends on numerous variable factors, including the personnel and equipment available.

TECHNOLOGICAL OBSOLESCENCE

Technological obsolesence is defined as the outdating and outpricing of technology-intensive products by innovation and rapid technological change. An example of the magnitude of this change is represented in Table 3.2, which compares the cost of doing 100,000 multiplications on a commercially available computer over a long time frame.

In addition to such rapid reduction in per-operation cost, similar im-

TABLE 3.2　COSTS OF
COMPUTATION.*

1952	$1.26
1958	0.26
1964	0.12
1970	0.05
1975	0.01

* 100,000 multiplications.

provements have been made in speed, size, reliability, and availability. While such lowered computational costs and wider availability makes possible new applications of computers, and more efficient utilization in existing applications, it also creates certain problems.

The basic problem of rapid technological obsolescence is the diminishing gap between marginal costs and marginal revenues. Expressed in another way, the difference between increased revenues from new applications, and decreased revenues from lower prices, is rapidly closing.

This basic problem of marginal costs/marginal revenues is not an academic issue, but has significant impact on the entire semiconductor industry, as well as technology-intensive product industries. Consider, for example, the effect of rapid technological change on the electronic calculator industry. Both the cost of the principal semiconductor components, as well as the selling price of the final assembled calculator, have decreased by more than a factor of 10 over a period of a few years. The impact of such rapid technological obsolescence was swift; in spite of a rapidly growing market, a number of calculator manufacturers, and even some calculator chip suppliers, underestimated the rapid technological change and consequential cost and price erosion. Under such conditions, a number of such manufacturers terminated their business.

The lesson the electronic calculator industry is significant for all technology-intensive product manufacturers, and particularly for manufacturers of products utilizing microprocessors, that are perhaps undergoing change and evolution more rapidly than most other components. The lesson goes beyond the simple conclusion that the microprocessor industry is highly competitive, and points to a broader redefinition of many industries.

Consider, for example, the design and fabrication of data terminals. In the past, manufacturers in this industry would purchase components and design a data terminal according to the desired specifications with the components. Now, most of the necessary functions are available in a handful of LSI components, and the "designing" task has been considerably diluted. Of course, with the designing options diluted, the possibility of creating a particularly unique and highly competitive product is also diminished. It is not surprising to see large-scale users of such terminals turn to the use of "custom" microprocessors, and even the development of in-house microprocessor development capabilities.

One final aspect of technological obsolescence to note is the concept of a technology saturation point. As the level of technological sophistication increases, technological innovation becomes more difficult and more expensive. At some point in development, a commercial saturation point will be reached at which further technological improvement would not be commercially justified. The word "commercial" should be emphasized here, since technology always continues to evolve in the research laboratory, and more advanced technologies may be implemented in military or special purpose applications. As the price of microprocessors drop below the $10.00 level, the saturation point is rapidly being approached.

Once the technology saturation point is reached, microprocessor manufacturers will begin directing their efforts to develop less technology-intensive products, such as software, to accompany their microprocessor systems. Indeed, many microprocessor manufacturers today are using the microprocessor as a "loss-leader" for selling more profitable memory and peripheral components in a complete system. This trend is expected to continue in the future, with even more offerings directed to making the microprocessor more simple and easy to use.

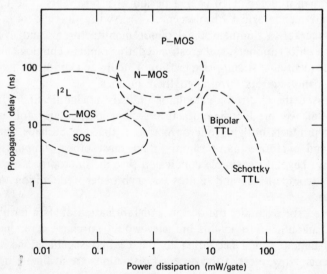

FIGURE 3.23 SPEED VERSUS POWER FOR SEMICONDUCTOR TECHNOLOGIES.

TECHNOLOGY COMPARISONS

Each of the semiconductor process technologies and circuit designs have different characteristics, advantages, and most suitable areas of application. The three most important characteristics are:

propagation delay
power dissipation
relative density

From these basic characteristics, the system designer can define two basic criteria:

speed versus power
density versus speed

Figures 3.23 and 3.24 present these criteria in terms of the average characteristics associated with the various process and circuit technologies.

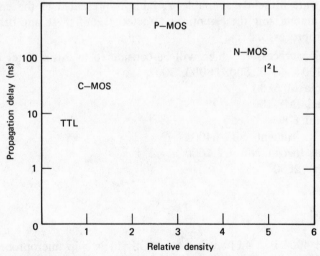

FIGURE 3.24 SPEED VERSUS DENSITY FOR SEMICONDUCTOR TECHNOLOGIES.

CHAPTER FOUR
MICROPROCESSOR
SURVEY

This chapter is a survey and overview of the basic architectures of some of the more widely known microprocessors. Over two dozen microprocessors are under development or commercially available today. It would be both impractical and unnecessary to describe each of these products in significant detail for the purposes of this introductory presentation. It is however useful to present the architectures of a few of these microprocessors to illustrate the wide range of capabilities and architectural designs that are presently available. A table is presented at the end of the chapter summarizing the essential characteristics of these and other available microprocessors.

The microprocessors which will be considered in this chapter are:
Intel 4004, 4040, 8008, 8080, 3002
Motorola M 6800
National IMP-16
Fairchild F-8
Texas Instruments SBP 0400
General Instruments CP-1600
Signetics 2650

INTEL 4004

The Intel 4004 is a 4-bit p-channel MOS single-chip microprocessor that was the first commercially available microprocessor, being made available in early 1971. Although the 4004 has been largely superceded by the Intel 4040, an improved 4-bit microprocessor that was announced in 1974, an examination of the architecture of the 4004 in comparison with the later 4040 is believed instructive.

The basic architecture of the 4004 is shown in Fig. 4.1, and a more detailed block diagram is presented in Fig. 4.2. Since the 4040 is essentially similiar to the 4004 structure, a description of the functional elements and operation is described in the section below on the 4040.

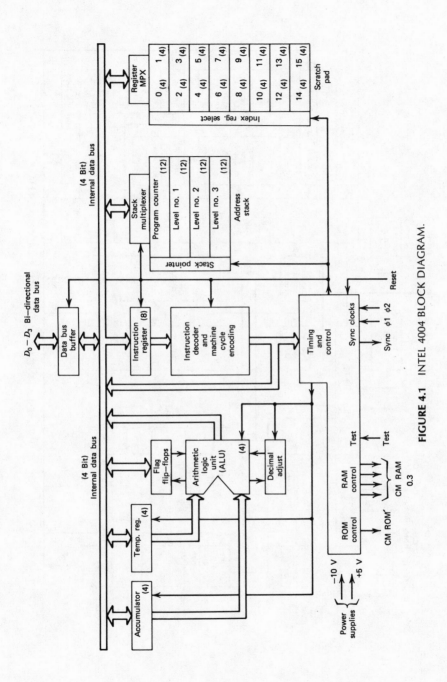

FIGURE 4.1 INTEL 4004 BLOCK DIAGRAM.

71

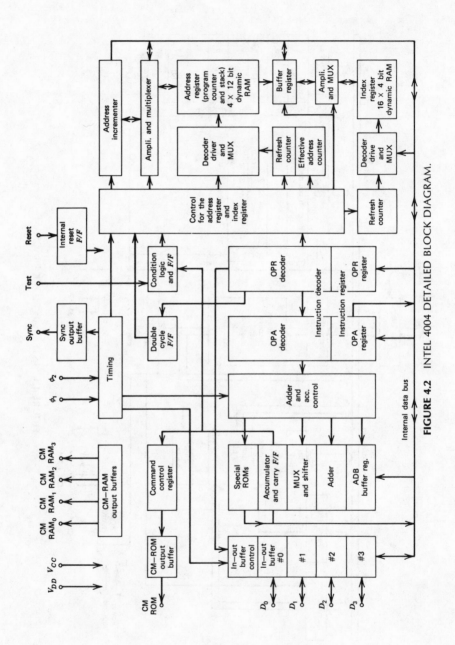

FIGURE 4.2 INTEL 4004 DETAILED BLOCK DIAGRAM.

72

A photomicrograph of the actual 4004 chip itself is shown in Fig. 4.3. Figure 4.4 is again the 4004, with an overlay to specify the various functional elements of the chip as shown in Fig. 4.2.

INTEL 4040

The Intel 4040 is a 4-bit *p*-channel MOS single-chip microprocessor. As a 4-bit unit, the 4040 is a relatively basic microprocessor intended for simple applications such as calculators, games, appliances, and other control applications.

The basic architecture of the 4040 is shown in Fig. 4.5. The CPU is organized around a single 4-bit internal data bus that interconnects the various internal registers of the machine. Input and output functions are performed by means of a 4-bit bidirectional data bus that interfaces with

FIGURE 4.3 INTEL 4004 (REPRINTED WITH PERMISSION, COPYRIGHT 1971 BY INTEL CORPORATION; ALL RIGHTS RESERVED).

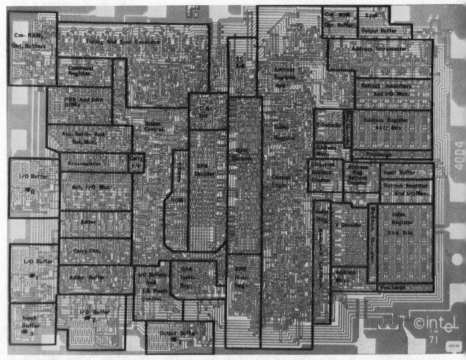

FIGURE 4.4 INTEL 4004 (REPRINTED WITH PERMISSION, COPYRIGHT 1971 BY INTEL CORPORATION; ALL RIGHTS RESERVED).

the four I/O pins of the 4040 package. The 4-bit data bus buffer holds the data being transferred between machine cycles.

The internal registers which are connected to the internal data bus are:

accumulator (4 bits)
temporary register (4 bits)
instruction register (8 bits)
8 address registers (4 bits)
12 index registers (8 bits)

The accumulator serves as a latch for storing data that are to be processored by the ALU, or for receiving such data that have already been processed. The temporary register is an internal register not under user control which temporarily stores data which have been transferred from another register.

The instruction register stores the next instruction to be executed by the processor. Instructions in the 4040 may be either one word (8 bits) or two words (16 bits) in length. The instruction register is 8 bits wide, so a one-word instruction is executed in one instruction cycle, while a two-word instruction is executed in two instruction cycles.

The address registers are designed to operate as a last-in first-out push-down stack. The address stack consists of a program counter and seven levels. The stack pointer points to the particular register which is considered to be the "top" of the stack. The address registers are 12 bits wide, so they must be multiplexed to the 4-bit internal data bus by means of a stack multiplexer.

The index registers are utilized for two purposes: as single 4-bit general-purpose registers; and second, in pairs, as 8-bit storage locations. The index registers may be used during interrupt processing for saving various status variables, as well as routinely during addressing to provide indexed addressing capabilities.

The instruction decoder and machine cycle encoding unit decodes the bit pattern of the instruction presented by the instruction register by translating it into the appropriate sequence of machine operations through the timing and control unit.

The timing and control unit controls all internal operations of the processor. The two-phase clock input is applied to this unit, and corresponding synchronization signals are transferred to the various internal elements of the processor. The unit also receives the external control signals such as "test," "interrupt," "stop," and "reset." The unit provides external control signals of "carry out," "ROM control," "RAM control," "stop acknowledge," and "synchronization."

INTEL 8008

The Intel 8008 is an 8-bit p-channel MOS single-chip microprocessor. The 8008, introduced in 1971, was the first 8-bit microprocessor to become commercially available and has since become incorporated in numerous microcomputer applications. Like the first microprocessor, Intel's 4004, the 8008 was originally designed as an OEM product for a manufacturer of CRT data terminals.

The architecture of the 8008 was based on the earlier 4004. Since Intel's newer 4-bit processor, the 4040, is also based on the architecture of the 4004, the similarities of the 8008 and the 4040 should be apparent from Fig. 4.6.

Like the 4040, the 8008 is organized around a single internal data bus, which in the case of the 8008 is 8 bits wide. Input and output functions are performed by means of an 8-bit bidirectional data bus which inter-

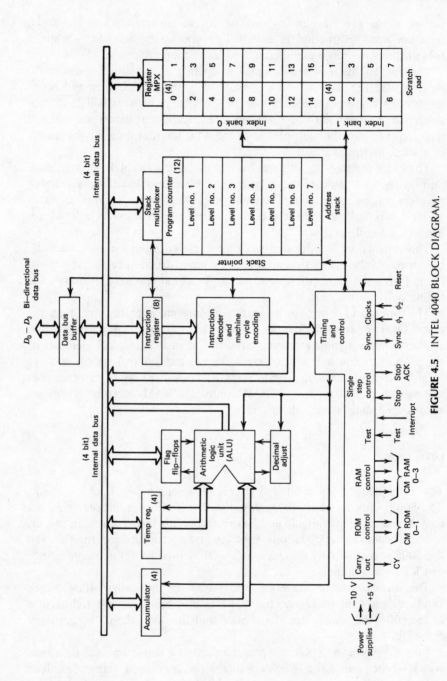

FIGURE 4.5 INTEL 4040 BLOCK DIAGRAM.

76

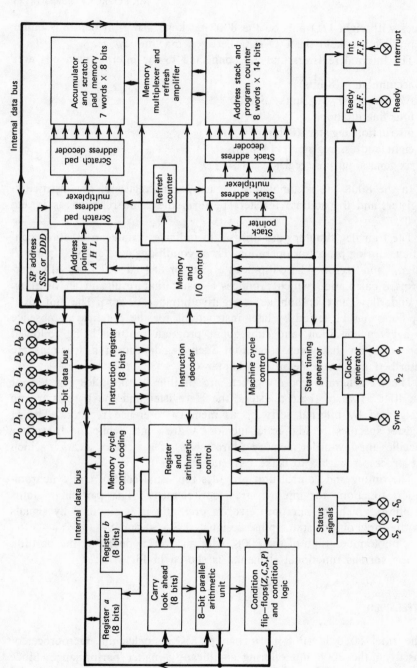

FIGURE 4.6 INTEL 8008 DETAILED BLOCK DIAGRAM.

77

faces with eight I/O pins on the 8008 package. An 8-bit data bus buffer is provided to hold the I/O data between machine cycles.

The internal registers that are connected to the internal data bus are:

accumulator (8 bits)
two temporary registers (8 bits)
four flag flip-flops
instruction register (8 bits)
eight address registers (14 bits)
six general-purpose registers (8 bits)

In the 8008 the accumulator, the temporary registers, the instruction register, and the address registers perform the same function as in the 4040.

The four flag flip-flops are utilized to indicate certain arithmetical conditions during processor operation. These conditions are "carry," "parity," "sign," and "zero." These flip-flops are set or flagged when the ALU performs a calculation which produces a result that results in an overflow or underflow, an even number, a negative number, or zero. The individual flip-flops may be tested by later instructions for the presence or absence of a given condition, and subsequent program routines being followed depending on that given condition. Such flag-dependent instructions are described in greater detail in Chapter 6.

The six general-purpose registers are similiar to the index registers of the 4040. Two of these registers, the H register and the L register, are designated by internal software as memory reference registers. The H register specifies the high-order memory address bits, while the L register specifies the low-order memory address bits, of a memory location which the processor wishes to make reference to.

The timing and control unit provides the usual control and synchronization functions for internal processor elements. The particular status or phase which the microprocessor is presently in is signified by signals on the three output status pins, designated S_0, S_1, and S_2.

A photomicrograph of the 8008, with an overlay depicting the position of the various functional elements, is shown in Fig. 4.7.

INTEL 8080

The Intel 8080 is an 8-bit n-channel MOS single-chip microprocessor based on the 8008 but offering significantly higher performance. Since there is a price differential between the two products, the 8080 should not be considered a replacement for the older 8008, but merely directed

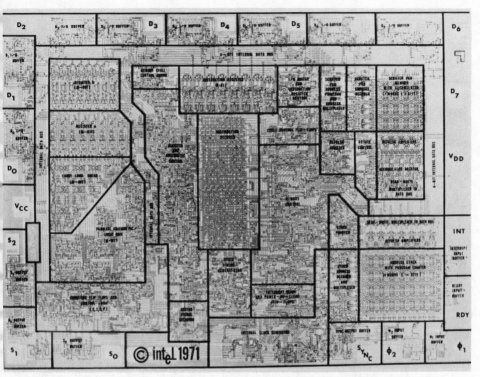

FIGURE 4.7 INTEL 8008 (REPRINTED WITH PERMISSION, COPYRIGHT 1971 BY INTEL CORPORATION; ALL RIGHTS RESERVED).

to more sophisticated applications that cannot be adequately handled by the 8008.

The architecture of the 8080 is shown in Fig. 4.8. Like the 8008, the 8080 is organized around a single 8-bit internal data bus. There are however several significant improvements:

external stack capability
direct memory access
decimal arithmetic
expanded instruction and addressing capabilities

One of the limitations of the 8008 was the limited stack depth, that is, seven levels corresponding to the seven address registers. Although few programs would actually make use of more than seven stack levels, the availability of an external stack offers greater design flexibility. The 8080 is therefore provided with an internal 16-bit stack pointer, which points

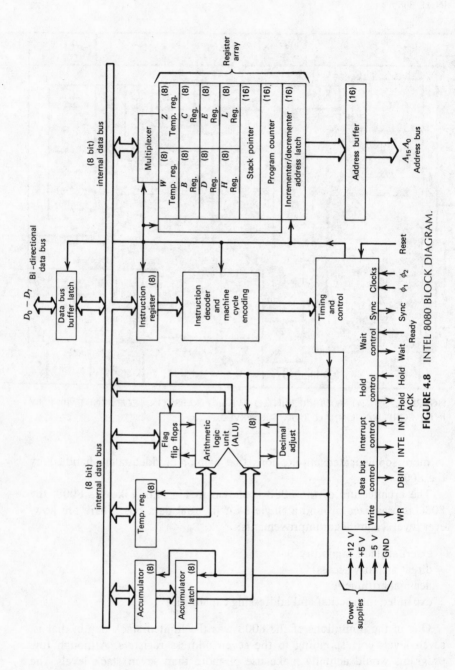

FIGURE 4.8 INTEL 8080 BLOCK DIAGRAM.

to an external memory address which is interpreted as the "top" of the stack.

Another important feature of the 8080 is the direct memory access capability. This capability is made possible by a "HOLD" input to the 8080. The HOLD capability suspends processor operation, thereby permitting the address and data busses of the system to be suspended in a floating state. External peripheral devices may now access the busses for direct data transfer without intervention or interference by processor operations.

Decimal arithmetic is a desirable feature for certain types of microcomputer applications. The 8080 features an instruction and a decimal adjust accumulator to translate the result of a floating point arithmetic operation into decimal format, that is, the representation of a number as two BCD digits separated by a decimal point.

The 8080 also has expanded instruction and addressing capabilities which enables more instructions to be performed, and more memory address locations to be accessed. A photomicrograph of the 8080 is shown in Fig. 4.9.

INTEL 3002

The Intel 3002 is a 2-bit-slice microprocessor based on Schottky bipolar technology. The 3002 Central Processing Element is implemented together with a 3001 Microprogram Control Unit (MCU) chip to form a two-chip microprocessor family based on user microcode stored in a microprogram memory.

A typical implementation of a 16-bit microcomputer using the 3001/ 3002 family is shown in Fig. 4.10. Eight 3002 Central Processing Elements are connected in an array to form a 16-bit CPU unit. The 3001 MCU addresses the microprogram memory which contains the user microcode. These selected microinstructions drive the 3002 array, perhaps through an optional pipeline register.

A better description of the operation of the 3001/3002 can be given with reference to functional block diagrams of the 3002 CPE and 3001 MCU. The 3002 CPE is shown in Fig. 4.11. There are three independent input buses to the processor:

M-bus, for memory data inputs
I-bus, for I/O data input
K-bus, for performing microprogram operations, such as masking

In addition, there are a number of control inputs. These include the

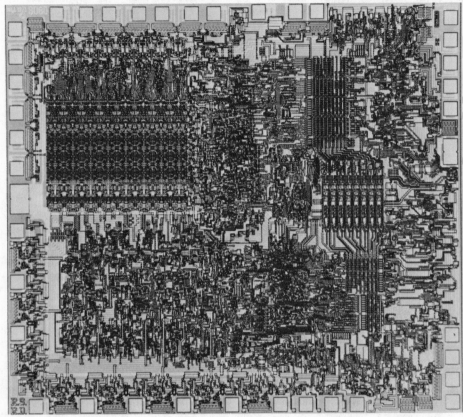

FIGURE 4.9 INTEL 8080 (REPRINTED WITH PERMISSION, COPYRIGHT 1973 BY INTEL CORPORATION; ALL RIGHTS RESERVED).

carry input (CI), a shift right input (LI), a memory address enable (EA), a data output enable (ED), and the microinstruction input $(F_0 - F_6)$.

The bus outputs of the 3002 CPE are:

A-bus, for memory address output
D-bus, for memory data output

In addition, there are carry look-ahead outputs (X,Y), a ripple carry output (CO), and a shift right output (RO).

The functional block diagram of the 3001 MCU is shown in Fig. 4.12. As the name "Microprogram Control Unit" implies, the function of the 3001 is to translate user instructions into microprogram control functions. This control is achieved by accessing specific sequences of row and col-

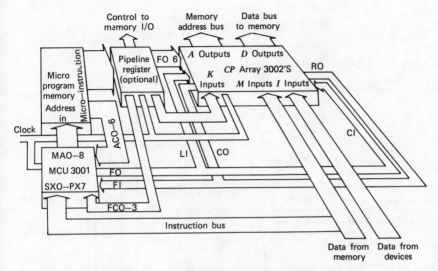

FIGURE 4.10   INTEL 3001/3002 MICROCOMPUTER.

umn addresses in the external ROM which contains the user microinstructions.

The user instructions to the 3001 MCU are typically provided from external memory along the X-bus. If a signal is provided along with microprogram address load input, the data on the X-but are loaded directly into the microprogram address register where it accesses the ROM directly. More typically, the user instruction is merely transferred to the Next Address Logic unit where it is handled in sequential order.

The other inputs applied to the 3001 MCU are flag logic control signals, a flag logic input, an enabling input for the microprogram address and other functions, and an enabling input for the row address outputs which may be used in priority interrupt systems.

The outputs of the 3001 MCU are connected to the microprogram memory, which is addressed in terms of predetermined rows and columns. Control outputs are also provided for modifying microinstructions, or for providing interrupt or flag indications.

MOTOROLA M 6800

The Motorola M 6800 is an 8-bit *n*-channel MOS single-chip microprocessor. The basic block diagram is shown in Fig. 4.13 and includes the following elements:

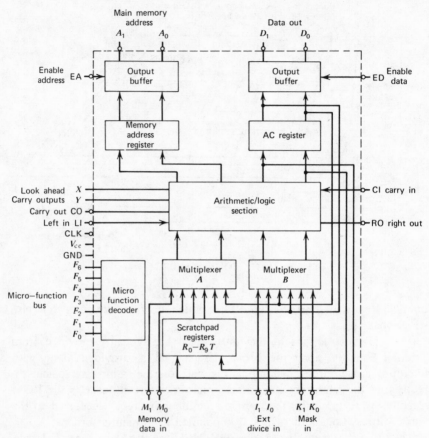

FIGURE 4.11   INTEL 3002 BLOCK DIAGRAM.

program counter (16 bit)
stack pointer (16 bit)
index register (16 bit)
two accumulators (8 bits)
condition code register

Each of these elements are connected to an internal 8-bit data bus. In addition, there is a 16-bit output address bus, and an 8-bit bidirectional I/O data bus.

In addition, a number of control functions are provided by means of I/O pins on the microprocessor. Some of the more important such control functions are:

halt—to halt processor operation.

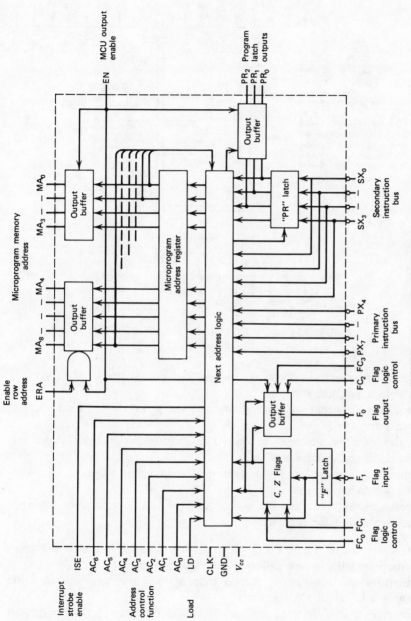

FIGURE 4.12 INTEL 3001 BLOCK DIAGRAM.

85

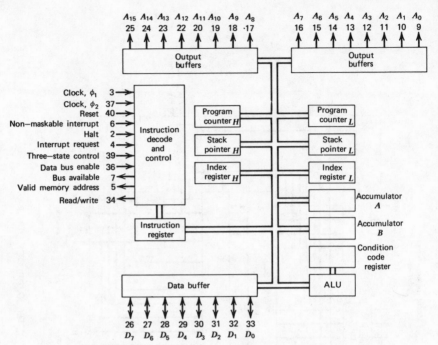

FIGURE 4.13   MOTOROLA M 6800 BLOCK DIAGRAM.

three-state control—to cause address and read/write lines to go into the high-impedence state.

read/write output—to signify whether the processor is in the read or write state.

valid memory address—an output indicating that a valid address is present on the address bus.

interrupt request input—to generate the interrupt sequence of operations within the processor.

nonmaskable interrupt input—to generate the nonmaskable interrupt sequence within the processor.

One feature of the M 6800 which is worth noting is that it processes instructions with several different addressing modes.

In *direct* addressing, the second byte of the instruction specifies the memory address of the operand.

In *extended* addressing, the second and third bytes of the instruction specify the memory address of the operand.

In *immediate* addressing, the second byte of the instruction is the data to be operated upon.

In *relative* addressing, the second byte of the instruction specifies the displacement from the memory location specified by the Program Counter.

In *indexed* addressing, the memory address of the operand is specified by the Index Register.

NATIONAL IMP-16

The National Semiconductor IMP-16 is a microcomputer family that may be constructed in a variety of configurations. The basic building blocks of the system are a single-chip register and arithmetic logic unit (RALU), and a single-chip Control and read-only memory (CROM).

The RALU is a four-bit "slice" unit: two RALUs must be connected in parallel to form an 8-bit unit, and four RALUs must be connected in parallel to form a 16-bit unit. The RALUs are controlled by microinstructions which are stored in one or two CROMs. These units are typically provided on a card, forming an 8-bit (IMP-8) or 16-bit (IMP-16) configuration.

The National RALU and CROM microprocessor utilizes *p*-channel MOS technology. Figure 4.14 illustrates the basic block diagram of the RALU. The RALU includes four status flags, a stack, seven registers, an ALU, a shifter, and an I/O data multiplexer.

The seven general-purpose registers (R1—R7) shown in the block diagram store a 4-bit word in each. A 16-word stack is also provided, along with a 4-bit status register for indicating conditions of link, overflow, carry, and flag. Control of the RALU is achieved over a 4-bit time multiplexed command bus. The ALU performs the operations of ADD, AND, OR and EXCLUSIVE OR on data from the registers. Data from the registers to the ALU is transferred along the A or the B bus, shown on the right hand side of the figure. A complementer is associated with the A bus to take the complement of the data on that bus before transfer to the ALU.

The output from the ALU is applied to a shifter which provides a 1-bit right, a 1-bit left, or no shift, to data on the S bus. Output data from the shifter may then be transferred to any of the registers via the R bus.

The basic block diagram of the CROM is shown in Fig. 4.15. The key element of the CROM is the read-only memory, which stores one hundred 23-bit microinstructions for use by the RALU. These microinstructions indicate the type of instruction, the particular registers to be loaded onto the A and B bus of the RALU, the ALU operation, the shift operation, and the register to be loaded from the R bus of the RALU.

The other elements of the CROM are concerned with ROM instruction

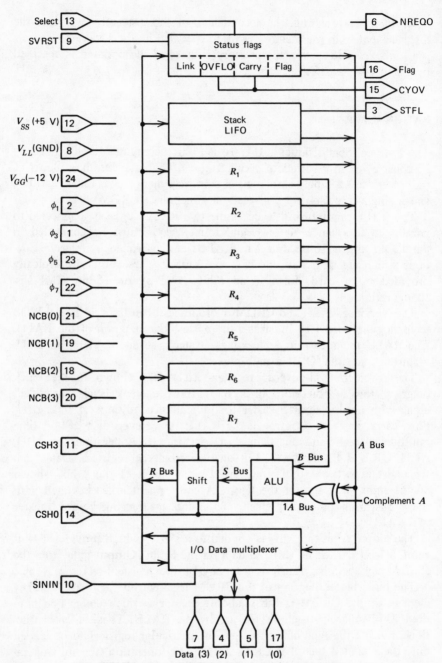

FIGURE 4.14 NATIONAL RALU BLOCK DIAGRAM.

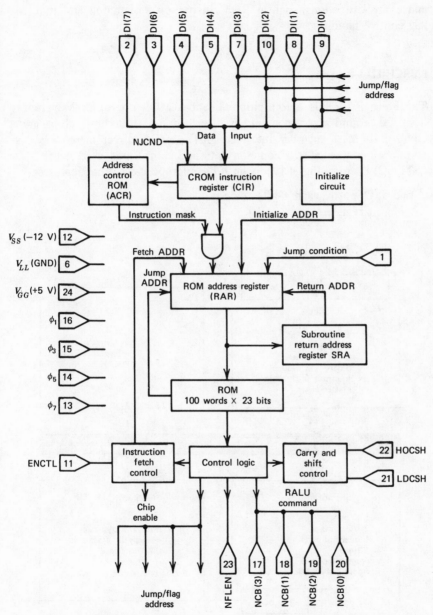

FIGURE 4.15 NATIONAL CROM BLOCK DIAGRAM.

and control functions, such as ROM insruction designation and jump or flag control handling.

FAIRCHILD F-8

The Fairchild F-8 is a four-chip *n*-channel MOS microprocessor family designed around a common bus architecture. The four basic chips are a CPU, a ROM, a memory interface (MI), and a direct memory access chip, each connected to a common data and control bus (Fig. 4.16).

The CPU chip (Fig. 4.17) is an 8-bit microprocessor that features

two I/O ports, each 8-bits wide
64 8-bit registers

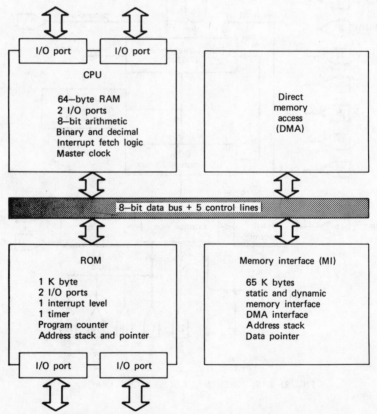

FIGURE 4.16 FAIRCHILD F-8 SYSTEM (COURTESY FAIRCHILD SEMICONDUCTOR COMPONENTS GROUP).

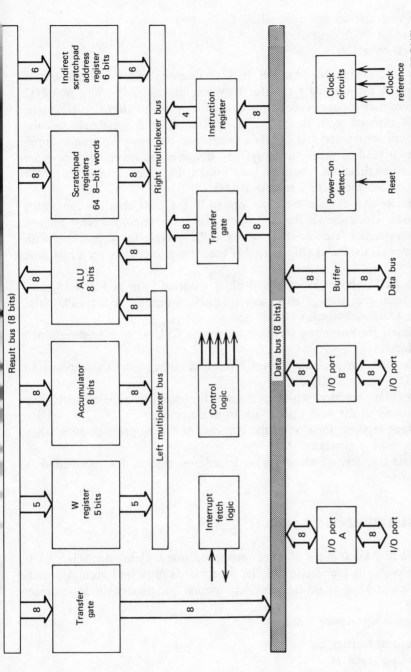

FIGURE 4.17 FAIRCHILD F-8 CPU BLOCK DIAGRAM (COURTESY FAIRCHILD SEMICONDUCTOR COMPONENTS GROUP).

clocking circuits for controlling the system
interrupt fetch controls
power-on detect

The architecture of the F-8 is I/O oriented, with internal busses adapted to expedite data transfer between internal units. The two I/O ports are bidirectional and simplify interfacing with external peripherals. The 64 internal registers serve as a workspace for doing simple calculations without transferring the data to external memory. For simple applications a random access memory may not even be necessary; for more complex applications, the user may utilize the memory interface (MI) chip for interfacing to standard RAMs.

The clocking circuits are incorporated in the CPU chip for generating two-phase clock signals for controlling the entire microprocessor system.

The interrupt fetch controls on the CPU operate in conjunction with the timer on the ROM chip to enable the system to operate on a real time basis.

The ROM, shown in simplified block diagram form in Fig. 4.18, provides additional storage and control functions outside of the CPU chip. These additional functions include:

a timer, for providing an interrupt to the CPU after a predetermined time interval

I/O ports, for providing direct input and output from the registers in the ROM under CPU control

a program counter, which performs the usual function of specifying the address of the next instruction in memory

a stack register, for storing the contents of the program counter when an interrupt is generated

a data counter, which serves as an address pointer for specified data in memory.

TEXAS INSTRUMENTS SBP 0400

The TI SBP 0400 is a 4-bit slice microprocessor utilizing nonisolated I²L technology. The architecture of the processor is organized around a multiple internal-bus structure, and an internal programmable logic array (PLA).

The microprocessor features:

a general register file
working registers
interface multiplexers

in addition to the internal programmable logic array.

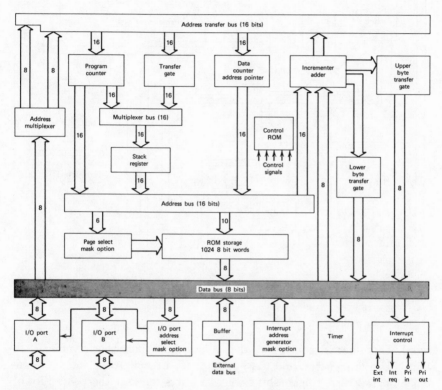

FIGURE 4.18 FAIRCHILD F-8 ROM BLOCK DIAGRAM (COURTESY FAIRCHILD SEMICONDUCTOR COMPONENTS GROUP).

The basic architecture of the SPB 0400 chip is shown in Fig. 4.19. (SBP stands for semiconductor bipolar processor). The key distinction of the SBP 0400 over other microprocessors is the replacement of the instruction register by the internal programmable logic array. The user may define an extensive instruction set that is unique to his particular requirements and write programs using such instructions. The user's instruction is represented as a 9-bit "operation select" word which is placed on a 9-pin input to the internal PLA. The PLA, operating under clock control, decodes this 9-bit input into the specific operations required by the user's instruction, which is represented by a 20-bit internal control

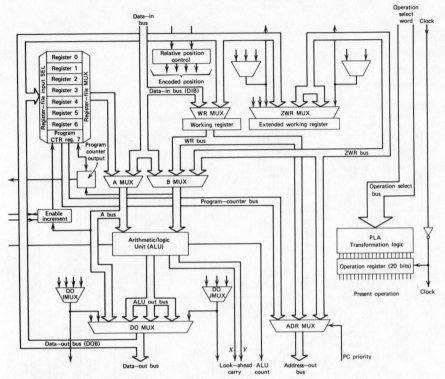

FIGURE 4.19   TEXAS INSTRUMENTS SBP 0400 BLOCK DIAGRAM.

word. This internal control word provides the appropriate commands to the ALU, the registers, and the bus lines for executing the intended machine operation. A single 4-bit slice unit offers the user the possibility of some 512 discrete machine operations which may be executed in a single clock cycle, which is considerably more than the instruction sets of other microprocessors.

The advantage of the programmed logic array in the SBP 0400 is two-fold: first, it offers greater system integrity and security. Since the PLA is programmed at the factory by the designer, it would be extremely difficult to "reverse-engineer" or attempt to copy the system. Designers who have invested considerable sums in software development may now ensure that their efforts remain proprietary by incorporating such programs in terms of "macroinstructions" utilizing the PLA. Since the operation register of the PLA is internal to the SBP 0400 chip, it would be utterly impractical for a user to attempt to decode the PLA structure by examining register contents and ALU operations for predetermined operation select word inputs. The second advantage of the PLA in the SBP 0400 is to permit emulation of larger scale computers having extended instruction sets. By appropriate coding the PLA such larger scale computers may be emulated without significant overhead or operation degradation.

Turning to the block diagram in Fig. 4.19 we note the two basic inputs to the ALU unit: a multiplexed A input port, and a multiplexed B input port. The data-in bus has access to either the A port, the B port, or the working register. The 8 general-purpose registers have access to the A port.

The output from the ALU is applied to a data output multiplexer (DO MUX), which transfer the data either externally of the chip or internally along the data-out bus (DOB) back to the general-purpose registers, working register, or extended working register.

GENERAL INSTRUMENT CP-1600

The General Instrument CP-1600 is a 16-bit n-channel ion-implant MOS single-chip microprocessor. The n-channel ion-implant technology makes the CP-1600 a relatively high-speed device, having a cycle time of 400 nanoseconds. The addition of two 16-bit numbers can be accomplished in 3.2 microseconds.

The relatively high performance of the CP-1600 makes the processor particularly suitable for high-speed real-time applications, such as terminals and process control systems.

The basic architecture of the CP-1600 is shown in Fig. 4.20. As illustrated in the figure, the system is organized around a 16-bit bidirectional data-bus. Connected to the bus are the following active elements:

a bidirectional I/O buffer
instruction register
ALU
eight general-purpose registers (16-bit)

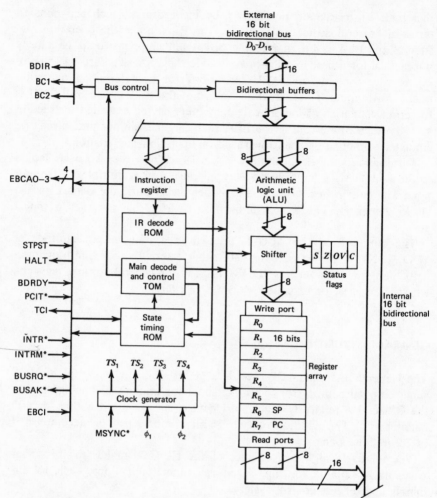

FIGURE 4.20   GENERAL INSTRUMENTS CP-1600 BLOCK DIAGRAM.

The instruction register is connected to an IR Decode ROM. The IR Decode ROM is an internal read-only memory which decodes the bit-sequence of the instruction in the instruction register to provide the appropriate control signals to the ALU, shifter, and general-purpose registers.

The ALU of the CP-1600 operates on 8-bit words. It processes two 8-bit words from the 16-bit bidirectional data bus and produces an 8-bit resultant, which is forwarded to the shifter. The shifter may shift the resultant one bit right or left or may perform no operation at all. The shifter also affects the status flags (Sign, Zero, Overflow, or Carry) depending on the resultant.

From the Shifter, the data enters the Write Port in which it may be transferred into any one of the eight general-purpose registers. The Read Port associated with the registers can then transfer 16-bits in the form of two 8-bit words from either one or two registers to the 16-bit bidirectional data bus.

The CP-1600 is driven by a two-phase clock at 5 megahertz, thus producing a cycle time of 400 nanoseconds as noted above. A state timing ROM decodes the state signals from external signals and transfers such information to the Main Decode and Control ROM. Some of these signals are as follows:

STPST: STOP START—a first transition used to stop the CPU after completion of an interruptable instruction followed by a second transition to start the CPU again.

BDRDY: BUS DATA READY—a signal used to resynchronize the CPU to slower peripherals by causing the CPU to wait.

PCIT*: PROGRAM COUNTER INHIBIT/TRAP*—a signal used to prevent the incrementing of the program counter during instruction execution; the pin may also be used in the output mode to indicate a software interrupt instruction.

INTR*: INTERRUPT REQUEST—an interrupt signal.

INTRM*: INTERRUPT REQUEST MASKABLE—an interrupt signal which is executed only if an internal interrupt flag is set.

The asterisked designation of certain input pins represents negative logic, that is, a low-level digital signal is operative for activation.

SIGNETICS 2650

The Signetics 2650 is an 8-bit n-channel ion-implant MOS single-chip microprocessor. The basic architecture of the 2650 is shown in the block diagram of Fig. 4.21.

As shown in the figure, the 2650 is organized around separate data and address busses. Seven 8-bit general-purpose registers are provided for data, as well as an eight-level stack for a subroutine return address. Among the other important features are a vectored interrupt capability and a flexible instruction set with up to eight different addressing modes.

Since the address capabilities is one of the more important features of the 2650, Fig. 4.22 presents the various instruction formats that may be used with the microprocessor.

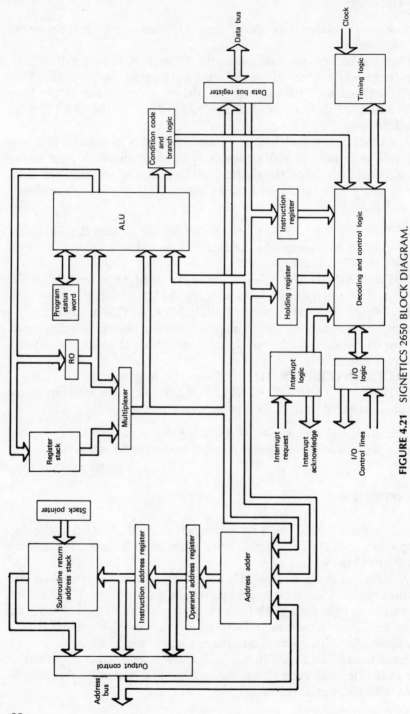

FIGURE 4.21 SIGNETICS 2650 BLOCK DIAGRAM.

98

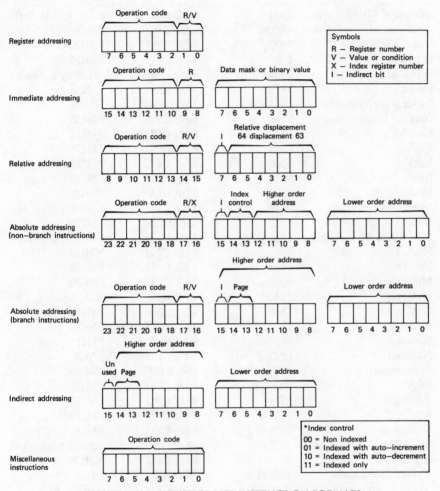

FIGURE 4.22 SIGNETICS 2650 INSTRUCTION FORMATS.

TABLE 4.1 MICROPROCESSORS.

Manufacturer	Designation	Classification	Technology
Advanced Micro Devices	2901	4-bit slice	Schottky Bipolar
American Microsystems	S9209	4-bit CPU	PMOS
Electronic Arrays	9002	8-bit CPU	NMOS
Fairchild	F-8	8-bit CPU	NMOS
Fairchild	9405	4-bit slice	Schottky Bipolar
Fairchild	34705	4-bit slice	CMOS
General Instruments	CP-1600	16-bit CPU	NMOS
General Instruments	LP-8000	8-bit CPU	PMOS
Hitachi		8-bit CPU	PMOS
Intel	4004	4-bit CPU	PMOS
Intel	4040	4-bit CPU	PMOS
Intel	8008	8-bit CPU	PMOS
Intel	8080	8-bit CPU	NMOS
Intel	3002	2-bit slice	Schottky Bipolar
Intersil	6100	12-bit CPU	CMOS
Monolithic Memories	6701	4-bit slice	Schottky Bipolar
MOS Technology	6501	8-bit CPU	NMOS
Mostek	5065	8-bit CPU	PMOS
Motorola	6800	8-bit CPU	NMOS
Motorola	10800	4-bit slice	ECL Bipolar
National	IMP-	4-bit slice	PMOS
National	PACE	16-bit CPU	PMOS
National	SC/MP	8-bit CPU	PMOS
National	CMP-8	8-bit CPU	NMOS
Panafacom	PFL-16A	16-bit CPU	NMOS
RCA	CDP1801	8-bit CPU	CMOS
Rockwell	PPS-4	4-bit CPU	PMOS
Rockwell	PPS-8	8-bit CPU	PMOS
Rockwell	PPS-4/2	4-bit CPU	PMOS
Scientific Micro Systems	SMS-300	16-bit CPU	Schottky Bipolar
Signetics	2650	8-bit CPU	NMOS
Texas Instruments	SBP0400	4-bit slice	I^2L
Texas Instruments	TMS1000	4-bit CPU	PMOS
Texas Instruments	TMS-9900	16-bit CPU	NMOS
Toshiba	TLCS-12	12-bit CPU	NMOS
Transitron	1601	4-bit slice	Schottky Bipolar
Western Digital	1621	16-bit CPU	NMOS

CHAPTER FIVE
MICROPROCESSOR OPERATION

The first requirement for microcomputer system design is a through understanding of the internal operations of the microprocessor. These include an analysis of the following:

instruction set
timing and synchronization
electrical specification
interfaces

In this chapter reference is made to the Intel 8080 microprocessor. The 8080 is chosen on the basis of its widespread popularity and availability and is meant to illustrate many features of microprocessors that are commerically available. Many of the architectural features of the 8080 are typical of 8-bit microprocessors, and the capabilities, advantages, and disadvantages of its operation are comparable to other products.

Before turning to an analysis of the instruction set and operation of the 8080 in detail, we first review the basic machine architecture.

8080 ARCHITECTURE

Although the basic block diagram of the architecture of the 8080 was presented in Chapter 4, it is again illustrated in Fig. 5.1 for completeness and consistency.

The 8080 is organized around an 8-bit internal data bus. Several basic elements are directly attached to the internal data bus:

a bidirectional I/O data bus
accumulator
temporary register
five flag flip-flops
instruction register
arithmetic logic unit
six general-purpose registers

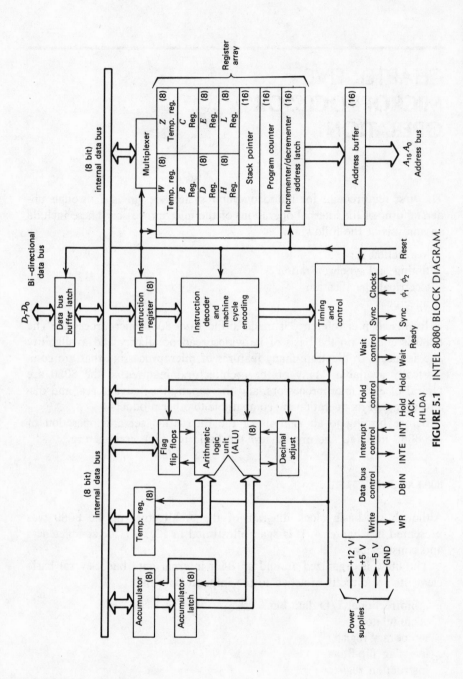

FIGURE 5.1 INTEL 8080 BLOCK DIAGRAM.

102

Also shown in the block diagram is the timing and control unit, and an address buffer associated with the 16-bit address bus.

The 8080 features six 8-bit general-purpose registers (labeled B, C, D, E, H, and L), and an 8-bit accumulator. As shown in the block diagram, the six general-purpose registers are arranged in pairs so that they may be addressed either singly for single precision operation or in pairs for double precision operation. Registers H and L are used for referencing memory. Register H refers to the eight High order bits of the memory address location, while register L refers to the eight Low order bits of the memory address location.

Like the Intel 8008, the 8080 permits an external stack in RAM to be referenced by a register on the chip. Since the stack may be located anywhere in the RAM, a 16-bit stack pointer register is provided in the 8080 for holding or "pointing to" the address of the top of the stack. A stack permits the use of programs with a large number of nested subroutines, or the implementation of multiple level priority interrupts, or other stack related operations. Since the stack is in RAM, the size of the stack is only limited by the amount of memory that many be addressed by the chip with the stack pointer.

Also shown in the block diagram is the 16-bit program counter. The program counter contains the address of the next instruction to the executed by the processor. The program counter is automatically updated and advanced by the processor during memory cycles.

A 16-bit incrementer/decrementer address latch is provided to store addresses associated with increment and decrement instructions.

Three 8-bit temporary registers are also shown in the block diagram. These are used internally by the processor for arithmetic operations and internal transfer of data. The register shown on the left side of the figure temporarily stores data during an internal machine cycle prior to be executed by the arithmetic logic unit. In a register to register transfer, for example, the data go from the first register to the temporary register, and then to the second register. The registers W and Z on the right-hand side of the figure are temporary registers associated with operations of the six general-purpose registers B, C, D, E. H and L. A multiplexer, shown in the block diagram directly above the register array on the right side of the figure, transfers the various registers to the internal data bus in a time multiplexed operation during double precision operations.

External memory is addressed by the 8080 by means of the Address Bus shown in the bottom right-hand side of the block diagram. A 16-bit address buffer is also provided for storing the address bits to be put out on the Address Bus. Since the address bus is 16-bits wide, up to 64K of 8-bits words in external memory may be directly accessed by the processor. Alternatively, the address lines may be organized by external logic to indicate a particular I/O device. In such a case, up to 256 input devices can be referenced by the processor.

At the bottom of the block diagram some of the control pins that are available on the 8080 are shown, connected to the timing and control unit. These control pins permit control signals to be transferred between the microprocessor and external logic devices which are provided by the designer.

Also shown is the representation of the external power that must be supplied to the processor: 12 volts, 5 volts, and −5 volts, as well as a ground connection. More information on the power requirements is provided in the section on Electrical Specifications.

The timing and control unit performs the internal function of sychronizing the various internal elements of the processor. The unit also performs control functions on the basis of control signals inputted to the processor from external logic and also provides external control signals through various output pins. The use of these control signals will become apparent from a detailed description of the pin function of the chip described below.

Communications of data between the microprocessor and external logic take place over an 8-bit bidirectional data bus. The data bus is connected to an 8-bit buffer or latch which captures the data on the data bus at appropriate points during the machine cycle. The 8-bit buffer is controlled by the timing and control unit to fully synchronize the I/O data bus with the internal data transfer operations.

Communications of data between the various internal registers of the microprocessor are achieved by a separate 8-bit internal data bus, shown as the horizontally extending line near the top of the block diagram. The timing and control unit specify which register will capture the data appearing on the internal data bus during appropriate points during the machine cycle.

The instruction register is one register that is connected to the internal data bus. At an appropriate point of the machine cycle an instruction code appears on the internal data bus, and the control unit indicates to the instruction register that the instruction should be "fetched." Once the instruction code is in the instruction register, the control unit then generates the basic signals necessary to decode the instruction in the instruction decoder and issue the necessary internal data transfer operations.

The 8080, like most other microprocessors, is internally microprogrammed. The internal microprogram acts to translate the instruction code into a sequence of microinstructions necessary to perform the arithmetic or logical operation required by the user. These microinstructions are internal to the microprocessor and are stored in an internal read-only memory. The nature of these microinstructions and the contents of the read-only memory are not accessible to the user, but it is not really necessary to know them. The ability to change the microinstructions or microcode is important only in a small number of critical applications, and for such applications Intel has supplied the 3000 series of microprogrammable microprocessors. Other microprocessor manufacturers also offer the capability of microprogramability in their products to permit the user to adapt the chip to a wider variety of instruction sets and applications.

The output from the instruction decoder and machine cycle encoding unit is transferred to the timing and control unit. The microinstructions operate to send appropriate signals to the various registers and ALU for performing the required operation. Such instructions may relate to reading or writing into any of the registers, changing the decimal adjust, and affecting the flag flip-flops (carry, zero, sign, and parity), all in connection with an arithmetic or logical operation performed in the ALU.

On the left-hand side of the block diagram is the accumulator, or A register. The accumulator is the principal register used in the various arithmetic or logical operations. Associated with the accumulator is an accumulator latch, for capturing and storing the contents of the accumulator.

INSTRUCTION SET

The 8080 microprocessor is operated by a sequence of instructions applied to the microprocessor from external logic or memory. Such instructions relate to the various operations that can be performed using the registers and I/O pins of the processor. These instructions can be grouped as follows:

register and memory transfers of data.
conditional and unconditional branches or subroutine calls.
I/O operations.
accumulator operations: load or store.
save or restore operations on registers, accumulator, and flags.
double precision operations in data registers: increment, decrement, addition; direct load or store; load immediate; register modification.
indirect jump.
logical operations.
arithmetic operations: binary and decimal.
flip-flop operations.
increment/decrement memory.

Figure 5.2 sets forth the instruction set for the 8080. The mnemonic is

Symbols	Meaning
\<B2\>	Second byte of the instruction
\<B3\>	Third byte of the instruction
r	One of the scratch pad register references: A, B, C, D, E, H, L
c	One of the following flag flip-flop references:

flag flip-flops.

Condition for True

carry — Overflow, underflow

zero — Result is zero

sign — MSB of result is "1"

parity — Parity of result is even

Symbols	Meaning
M	Memory location indicated by the contents of registers H and L
( )	Contents of location or register
Λ	Logical product
V	Exclusive "or"
$\underline{V}$	Inclusive "or"
r_m	Bit m of register r
SP	Stack Pointer
PC	Program Counter
$\leftarrow$	Is transferred to
XXX	A "don't care"
SSS	Source register for data
DDD	Destination register for data

Register # (SSS or DDD)	Register Name
000	B
001	C
010	D
011	E
100	H
101	L
110	Memory
111	ACC

8080
INSTRUCTION SET

Mnemonic	Bytes	Cycles	Description of operation
MOV r_1, r_2	1	1	$(r_1) \leftarrow (r_2)$ Load register r_1 with the content of r_2. The content of r_2 remains unchanged.
MOV r, M	1	2	$(r) \leftarrow (M)$ Load register r with the content of the memory location addressed by the contents of registers H and L.
MOV M, r	1	2	$(M) \leftarrow (r)$ Load the memory location addressed by the contents of registers H and L with the content of register r.
MVI r \<B₂\>	2	2	$(r) \leftarrow \langle B_2 \rangle$ Load byte two of the instruction into register r.
MVI M \<B₂\>	2	3	$(M) \leftarrow \langle B_2 \rangle$ Load byte two of the instruction into the memory location addressed by the contents of registers H and L.

Mnemonic	Bytes	Cycles	Description of operation
INR r	1	1	$(r) \leftarrow (r) + 1$ The content of register r is incremented by one. All the condition flip-flops except carry are affected by the result.
DCR r	1	1	$(r) \leftarrow (r) - 1$ The content of register r is decremented by one. All of the condition flip-flops except carry affected by the result.
ADD r	1	1	$(A) \leftarrow (A) + (r)$ Add the content of register r to the content of register A and place the result into register A. (All flags affected.)
ADC r	1	1	$(A) \leftarrow (A) + (r) + (carry)$ Add the content of register r and the contents of the carry flip-flop to the content of the A register and place the result into register A. (All flags affected.)
SUB r	1	1	$(A) \leftarrow (A) - (r)$ Subtract the content of register r from the content of register A and place the result into register A. Two's complement subtraction is used. (All flags affected.)
SBB r	1	1	$(A) \leftarrow (A) - (r) - (borrow)$ Subtract the content of register r and the content of the carry flip-flop from the content of register A and place the result into register A. (All flags affected.)
ANA r	1	1	$(A) \leftarrow (A) \wedge (r)$ Place the logical product of the register A and register r into register A. (Resets carry.)
XRA r	1	1	$(A) \leftarrow (A) \vee (r)$ Place the "exclusive-or" of the content of register A and register r into register A. (Resets carry.)
ORA r	1	1	$(A) \leftarrow (A) \veebar (r)$ Place the "inclusive-or" of the content of register A and register r into register A. (Resets carry.)
CMP r	1	1	$(A) - (r)$ Compare the content of register A with the content of register r. The content of register A remains unchanged. The flag flip-flops are set by the result of the subtraction. Equality $(A = r)$ is indicated by the zero flip-flop set to "1." Less than $(A < r)$ is indicated by the carry flip-flop, set to "1."
ADD M	1	2	$(A) \leftarrow (A) + (M)$ ADD
ADC M	1	2	$(A) \leftarrow (A) + (M) + (carry)$ ADD with carry
SUB M	1	2	$(A) \leftarrow (A) - (M)$ SUBTRACT
SBB M	1	2	$(A) \leftarrow (A) - (M) - (borrow)$ SUBTRACT with borrow
ANA M	1	2	$(A) \leftarrow (A) \wedge (M)$ Logical AND
XRA M	1	2	$(A) \leftarrow (A) \vee (M)$ Exclusive OR
ORA M	1	2	$(A) \leftarrow (A) \veebar (M)$ Inclusive OR
CMP M	1	2	$(A) - (M)$ COMPARE
ADI $<B_2>$	2	2	$(A) \leftarrow (A) + <B_2>$ ADD
ACI $<B_2>$	2	2	$(A) \leftarrow (A) + <B_2> + (carry)$ ADD with carry
SUI $<B_2>$	2	2	$(A) \leftarrow (A) - <B_2>$ SUBTRACT
SBI $<B_2>$	2	2	$(A) \leftarrow (A) - <B_2> - (borrow)$ SUBTRACT with borrow
ANI	2	2	$(A) \leftarrow (A) \wedge <B_2>$

(M) addressed by the contents of registers H and L. Flags affected are same as nonmemory reference instructions.

Mnemonic	Bytes	Cycles	Description of operation
$<B_2>$			Logical AND
XRI	2	2	$(A) \leftarrow (A)$ $<B_2>$
$<B_2>$			Exclusive OR
ORI	2	2	$(A) \leftarrow (A)$ $<B_2>$
$<B_2>$			Inclusive OR
CPI	2	2	$(A) - <B_2>$
$<B_2>$			COMPARE
RLC	1	1	$A_{m+1} \leftarrow A_m, A_0 \leftarrow A_7, (carry) \leftarrow A_7$ Rotate the content of register A left one bit. Rotate A_7 into A_0 and into the carry flip-flop.
RRC	1	1	$A_m \leftarrow A_{m+1}, A_0 (carry) \leftarrow A_0$ Rotate the content of register A right one bit. Rotate A_0 into A_7 and into the carry flip-flop.
RAL	1	1	$A_{m+1} \leftarrow A_m, A_0 \leftarrow (carry), (carry) \leftarrow A_7$ Rotate the content of register A left one bit. Rotate the content of the carry flip-flop into A_7. Rotate A_7 into the carry flip-flop.
RAR	1	1	$A_m \leftarrow A_{m+1}, A_7 \leftarrow (carry), carry) \leftarrow A_0$ Rotate the content of the carry flip-flop into A_0. Rotate the content of register A right one bit. Rotate A_0 into the carry flip-flop.
JMP $<B_2>$ $<B_3>$	3	3	$(PC) \leftarrow <B_3> <B_2>$ Jump unconditionally to the instruction located in memory location addressed by byte two and byte three.
JC $<B_2>$ $<B_3>$	3	3	If $(Carry) = 1 (PC) \leftarrow <B_3> <B_2>$ Otherwise $(PC) = (PC) + 3$
JNC $<B_2>$ $<B_3>$	3	3	If $(Carry) = 0 (PC) \leftarrow <B_3> <B_2>$ Otherwise $(PC) = (PC) + 3$
JZ $<B_2>$ $<B_3>$	3	3	If $(Zero) = 1 (PC) \leftarrow <B_3> <B_2>$ Otherwise $(PC) = (PC) + 3$
JNZ $<B_2>$ $<B_3>$	3	3	If $(Zero) = 0 (PC) \leftarrow <B_3> <B_2>$ Otherwise $(PC) = (PC) + 3$
JP $<B_2>$ $<B_3>$	3	3	If Sign) $= 0 (PC) \leftarrow <B_3> <B_2>$ Otherwise $(PC) = (PC) + 3$
JM $<B_2>$ $<B_3>$	3	3	If $(Sign) = 1 (PC) \leftarrow <B_3> <B_2>$ Otherwise $(PC) = (PC) + 3$
JPE $<B_2>$ $<B_3>$	3	3	If $(Parity) = 1 (PC) \leftarrow <B_3> <B_2>$ Otherwise $(PC) = (PC) + 3$
JPO $<B_2>$ $<B_3>$	3	3	If $(Parity) = 0 (PC) \leftarrow <B_3> <B_2>$ Otherwise $(PC) = (PC) + 3$
HLT	1	1	On receipt of the Halt Instruction, the activity of the processor is immediately suspended in the STOPPED

Mnemonic	Bytes	Cycles	Description of operation
			state. The content of all registers and memory is unchanged and the PC has been updated.
CALL $<B_2>$ $<B_3>$	3	5	$[SP-1]$ $[SP-2] \leftarrow (PC)$, $(SP) = (SP)-2$ $(PC) \leftarrow <B_3> <B_2>$ Transfer the content of PC to the pushdown stack in memory addressed by the register SP. The content of SP is decremented by two. Jump unconditionally to the instruction located in memory location addressed by byte two and byte three of the instruction.
CC $<B_2>$ $<B_3>$	3	3/5	If (carry) $=1$ $[SP-1]$ $[SP-2] \leftarrow PC$, $(SP) = (SP)-2$, $(PC) \leftarrow <B_3> <B_2>$; otherwise $(PC) = (PC)+3$
CNC $<B_2>$ $<B_3>$	3	3/5	If (carry) $=0$ $[SP-1]$ $[SP-2] \leftarrow PC$, $(SP) = (SP)-2$, $(PC) \leftarrow <B_3> <B_2>$; otherwise $(PC) = (PC)+3$
CZ $<B_2>$ $<B_3>$	3	3/5	If (zero) $=1$ $[SP-1]$ $[SP-2] \leftarrow PC$, $(SP) = (SP)-2$, $(PC) \leftarrow <B_3> <B_2>$; otherwise $(PC) = (PC)+3$
CNZ $<B_2>$ $<B_3>$	3	3/5	If (zero) $=0$ $[SP-1]$ $[SP-2] \leftarrow PC$, $(SP) = (SP)-2$, $(PC) \leftarrow <B_3> <B_2>$; otherwise $(PC) = (PC)+3$
CP $<B_2>$ $<B_3>$	3	3/5	If (sign) $=0$ $[SP-1]$ $[SP-2] \leftarrow PC$, $(SP) = (SP)-2$, $(PC) \leftarrow <B_3> <B_2>$; otherwise $(PC) = (PC)+3$
CM $<B_2>$ $<B_3>$	3	3/5	If (sign) $=1$ $[SP-1]$ $[SP-2] \leftarrow PC$, $(SP) = (SP)-2$, $(PC) \leftarrow <B_3> <B_2>$; otherwise $(PC) = (PC)+3$
CPE $<B_2>$ $<B_3>$	3	3/5	If (parity) $=1$ $[SP-1]$ $[SP-2] \leftarrow PC$, $(SP) = (SP)-2$, $(PC) \leftarrow <B_3> <B_2>$; otherwise $(PC) = (PC)+3$
CPO $<B_2>$ $<B_3>$	3	3/5	If (parity) $=0$ $[SP-1]$ $[SP-2] \leftarrow PC$, $(SP) = (SP)-2$, $(PC) \leftarrow <B_3> <B_2>$; otherwise $(PC) = (PC)+3$
RET	1	3	$(PC) \leftarrow [SP]$ $[SP+1]$ $(SP) = (SP)+2$. Return to the instruction in the memory location addressed by the last values shifted into the pushdown stack addressed by SP. The content of SP is incremented by two.
RC	1	1/3	If (carry) $=1$ $(PC) \leftarrow [SP]$, $[SP+1]$, $(SP) = (SP)+2$; otherwise $(PC) = (PC)+1$
RNC	1	1/3	If (carry) $=0$ $(PC) \leftarrow [SP]$, $[SP+1]$, $(SP) = (SP)+2$; otherwise $(PC) = (PC)+1$
RZ	1	1/3	If (zero) $=1$ $(PC) \leftarrow [SP]$, $[SP+1]$, $(SP) = (SP)+2$; otherwise $(PC) = (PC)+1$
RNZ	1	1/3	If (zero) $=0$ $(PC) \leftarrow [SP]$, $[SP+1]$, $(SP) = (SP)+2$; otherwise $(PC) = (PC)+1$

Mnemonic	Bytes	Cycles	Description of operation
RP	1	1/3	If (sign) =0 (PC)←[SP], [SP+1], (SP) = (SP) +2; otherwise (PC) = (PC) +1
RM	1	1/3	If (sign) =1 (PC)←[SP], [SP+], (SP) = (SP) +2; otherwise (PC) = (PC) +1
RPE	1	1/3	If (parity) =1 (PC)←[SP], [SP+1], (SP) = (SP) +2; otherwise (PC) = (PC) +1
RPO	1	1/3	If (parity) =0 (PC)←[SP], [SP+1], (SP) = (SP) +2; otherwise (PC) = (PC) +1
RST	1	3	[SP−1] [SP−2]←(PC), (SP) = (SP) −2 (PC)←(00000000 00AAA000)
IN $<B_2>$	2	3	(A) ←(Input data) At T_1 time of third cycle, byte two of the instruction, which denotes the I/O device number, is sent to the I/O device through the address lines*, and the INP status information, instead of MEMR, is sent out at sync time. New data for the accumulator are loaded from the data but when DBIN control signal is active. The condition flip-flops are not affected.
OUT $<B_2>$	2	3	(Output data) ←(A) At T_1 time of the third cycle, byte two of the instruction, which denotes the I/O device number, is sent to the I/O device through the address lines*, and the OUT status information is sent out at sync time. The content of the accumulator is made available on the data but when the $\overline{WR}$ control signal is 0.
LXI B $<B_2>$ $<B_3>$	3	3	(C)←$<B_2>$; (B) ←$<B_3>$ Load byte two of the instruction into C. Load byte three of the instruction into B.
LXI D $<B_2>$ $<B_3>$	3	3	(E) ←$<B_2>$, (D)←$<B_3>$ Load byte two of the instruction into E. Load byte three of the instruction into D.
LXI H $<B_2>$ $<B_3>$	3	3	(L) ←$<B_2>$, (H)←$<B_3>$ Load byte two of the instruction into L. Load byte three of the instruction into H.
LXI SP $<B_2>$ $<B_3>$	3	3	$(SP)_L$ ←$<B_2>$, $(SP)_H$ ←$<B_3>$ Load byte two of the instruction into the lower order 8-bit of the stack pointer and byte three into the higher order 8-bit of the stack pointer.
PUSH PSW	1	3	[SP−1]←(A), [SP−2]←(F), (SP) = (SP) −2 Save the contents of A and F (5-flags) into the pushdown stack addressed by the SP register. The content of SP is decremented by two. The flag word will appear as follows: D_0: CY_2 (Carry) D_1: 1

Mnemonic	Bytes	Cycles	Description of operation
			D_2: Parity (even)
			D_3: 0
			D_4: CY_1
			D_5: 0
			D_6: Zero
			D_7: MSB (sign)
PUSH B	1	3	$[SP-1] \leftarrow (B)$ $[SP-2] \leftarrow (C)$, $(SP) = (SP) - 2$
PUSH D	1	3	$[SP-1] \leftarrow (D)$ $[SP-2] \leftarrow (E)$, $(SP) = (SP) - 2$
PUSH H	1	3	$[SP-1] \leftarrow (H)$ $[SP-2] \leftarrow (L)$, $(SP) = (SP) - 2$
POP PSW	1	3	$(F) \leftarrow [SP]$, $(A) \leftarrow [SP+1]$, $(SP) = (SP) + 2$
			Restore the last values in the pushdown stack addressed by SP into A and F. The content of SP is incremented by two.
POP B	1	3	$(C) \leftarrow [SP]$, $(B) \leftarrow [SP+1]$, $(SP) = (SP) + 2$
POP D	1	3	$(E) \leftarrow [SP]$, $(D) \leftarrow [SP+1]$, $(SP) = (SP) + 2$
POP H	1	3	$(L) \leftarrow [SP]$, $(H) \leftarrow [SP+1]$, $(SP) = (SP) + 2$
STA $<B_2>$ $<B_3>$	3	4	$[<B_3> <B_2>] \leftarrow (A)$ Store the accumulator content into the memory location addressed by byte two and byte three of the instruction.
LDA $<B_2>$ $<B_3>$	3	4	$(A) \leftarrow [<B_3> <B_2>]$ Load the accumulator with the content of the memory location addressed by byte two and byte three of the instruction.
XCHG	1	1	$(H) \leftarrow \rightarrow (D)$ $(E) \leftarrow \rightarrow (L)$ Exchange the contents of registers H and L and registers D and E.
XTHL	1	5	$(L) \leftarrow \rightarrow [SP]$, $(H) \leftarrow \rightarrow [SP+1]$ Exchange the contents of registers H, L and the last values in the pushdown stack addressed by registers SP. The SP register itself is not changed. $(SP) = (SP)$
SPHL	1	1	$(SP) \leftarrow (H) (L)$ Transfer the contents of registers H and L into register SP.
PCHL	1	1	$(PC) \leftarrow (H) (L)$ JUMP INDIRECT
DAD SP	1	3	$(H) (L) \leftarrow (H) (L) + (SP)$ Add the content of register SP to the content of registers H and L and place the result into registers H and L. If the overflow is generated, the carry flip-flop is set; otherwise, the carry flip-flop is reset. The other condition flip-flops are not affected. This is useful for addressing data in the stack.
DAD B	1	3	$(H) (L) \leftarrow (H) (L) + (B) (C)$
DAD H	1	3	$(H) (L) \leftarrow (H) (L) + (H) (L)$ (double precision shift left H and L)
DAD D	1	3	$(H) (L) \leftarrow (H) (L) + (D) (E)$
STAX B	1	2	$[(B) (C)] \leftarrow (A)$ Store the accumulator content in the memory location addressed by the content of registers B and C.
STAX D	1	2	$[(D) (E)] \leftarrow (A)$ Store the accumulator content into the memory location addressed by the content of register D and E.

Mnemonic	Bytes	Cycles	Description of operation
LDAX B	1	2	(A)←[(B) (C)] Load the accumulator with the content of the memory location addressed by the content of registers B and C.
LDAX D	1	2	(A)←[(D) (E)] Load the accumulator with the content of memory location addressed by the content of register D and E.
INX B	1	1	(B) (C)←(B) (C)+1 The content of register pair B and C is incremented by one. All of the condition flip-flops are not affected.
INXH	1	1	(H) (L)←(H) (L)+1 The content of register H and L is incremented by one. All of the condition flip-flops are not affected.
INX D	1	1	(D) (E)←(D) (E)+1
INX SP	1	1	(SP)←(SP)+1
DCX B	1	1	(B) (C)←(B) (C)−1
DCX H	1	1	(H) (L)←(H) (L)−1
DCX D	1	1	(D) (E)←(D) (E)−1
DCX SP	1	1	(SP)←(SP)−1
CMA	1	1	(A)←$\overline{(A)}$ The content of accumulator is complemented. The condition flip-flops are not affected.
STC	1	1	(Carry)←1 Set the carry flip-flop to 1. The other condition flip-flops are not affected.
CMC	1	1	(carry)←($\overline{\text{carry}}$) The content of carry is complemented. The other condition flip-flops are not affected.
DAA	1	1	Decimal Adjust Accumulator The 8-bit value in the accumulator containing the result from an arithmetic operation on decimal operands is adjusted to contain two valid BCD digits by adding a value according to the following rules:

$$7 \rule{1cm}{0.4pt} 4 \quad 3 \rule{1cm}{0.4pt} 0$$

X	Y

Accumulator

If $(Y \geq 10)$ of (carry from bit 3) then $Y = Y + 6$ with carry to X digit.
If $(X \geq 10)$ or (carry from bit 7) or $[(Y \geq 10)$ and $(X = 9)]$ then $X = X + 6$ (which sets the carry flip-flop). Two carry flip-flops are used for this instruction. CY_1 represents the carry from bit 3 (the fourth bit) and is accessible as a fifth flag. CY_2 is the carry from bit 7 and is the usual carry bit.
All condition flip-flops are affected by this instruction.

Mnemonic	Bytes	Cycles	Description of operation
SHLD <B_2> <B_3>	3	5	[<B_1> <B_2>]←(L), [<B_3> <B_2>+1]←(H) Store the contents of registers H and L into the memory location addressed by byte two and byte three of the instructions.
LHLD <B_2>	3	5	(L)←[<B_3> <B_2>], (H)←[<B_3> <B_2>+1] Load the registers H and L with the contents of the

Mnemonic	Bytes	Cycles	Description of operation
$<B_3>$			memory location addressed by byte two and byte three of the instruction.
EI	1	1	Interrupt System Enable
DI	1	1	Interrupt System Disable
			The Interrupt Enable flip-flop (INTE) can be set or reset by using the above mentioned instructions. The INT signal will be accepted if the INTE is set. When the INT signal is accepted by the CPU, the INTE will be reset immediately. During interrupt enable or disable instruction executions, an interrupt will not be accepted.
INR M	1	3	$[M] \leftarrow [M] + 1$. The content of memory designated by registers H and L is incremented by one. All of the condition flip-flops except carry are affected by the result.
DCR M	1	3	$[M] \leftarrow [M] - 1$. The content of memory designated by registers H and L is decremented by one. All of the condition flip-flops except carry are affected by the result.

* The device address appears on $A_7 - A_0$ and $A_{15} - A_8$.

FIGURE 5.2 8080 INSTRUCTION SET (REPRINTED BY PERMISSION FROM *8080 MICROCOMPUTER SYSTEM MANUAL*, COPYRIGHT 1975, INTEL CORPORATION.)

merely a method of representing the instruction in a form that is easy to remember and facilitates actual programming. Such symbolic code may be translated into the binary bit pattern by an appropriate assembler. Such software techniques are discussed in a later chapter and are not of concern here.

Also indicated is the number of bytes (1, 2, or 3) which the instruction occupies in memory. Such numbers are important if one is concerned about minimizing the amount of memory space a program takes. The number of cycles for execution of the instruction is also indicated, along with a detailed description of the operation.

TIMING AND SYNCHRONIZATION

The timing and sychronization of the microprocessor with other system elements is one of the most fundamental and critical aspects of microcomputer system design. Microprocessors, like general-purpose computers, are synchronous sequential machines and therefore perform a specified sequence of operations during consecutive portions of a machine cycle. The specific sequence of operations is governed by the flow chart illustrated in Fig. 5.3.

Each instruction executed by the microprocessor takes from one to five

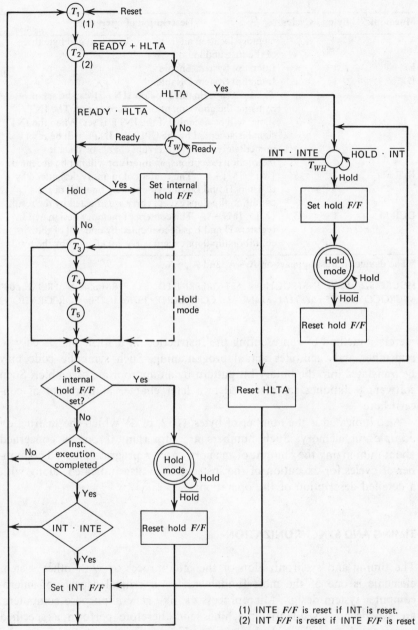

Reset

T_1
(1)

T_2
(2)

$\overline{\text{READY}} + \text{HLTA}$

HLTA — Yes

READY · $\overline{\text{HLTA}}$

No

Ready — T_W — $\overline{\text{Ready}}$

INT · INTE — T_{WH} — $\overline{\text{HOLD}} · \overline{\text{INT}}$

Hold — Yes — Set internal hold F/F

No

Hold

Set hold F/F

T_3

T_4

Hold
mode — Hold

$\overline{\text{Hold}}$

T_5

Hold
mode

Reset hold F/F

Is
internal
hold F/F
set? — Yes

No

Reset HLTA

Inst.
execution
completed — No

Hold
mode — Hold

$\overline{\text{Hold}}$

Yes

INT · INTE

Reset hold F/F

Yes

Set INT F/F

(1) INTE F/F is reset if INT is reset.
(2) INT F/F is reset if INTE F/F is reset

FIGURE 5.3 8080 STATE TRANSITION DIAGRAM.

114

machine cycles for fetching and execution. The amount of time an instruction execution takes depends on the number of bytes in the instruction, as well as the nature of the instruction itself. The execution time in number of machine cycles is given for each instruction in the section on Instruction Set.

Each machine cycle is in turn composed of from three to five *states*. These states are labeled T_1, T_2, T_3, T_4, T_5, and are represented as circles in the State Transition Diagram or flow chart Fig. 5.3.

The actual specification of the various states with respect to the two clock pulses is explictly shown in Fig. 5.4, the timing diagram. For completeness the timing diagram also shows a sixth or wait state represented by T_w. The timing diagram also shows the activation or logical levels of various data or control lines of the microprocessor during each state.

A detailed description of the microprocessor operation can now be made with reference to Figs. 5.3 and 5.4.

The top two rows of Fig. 5.4 illustrates the nonoverlapping clock pulses. It should be immediately evident that the pulsewidth of the ϕ_2

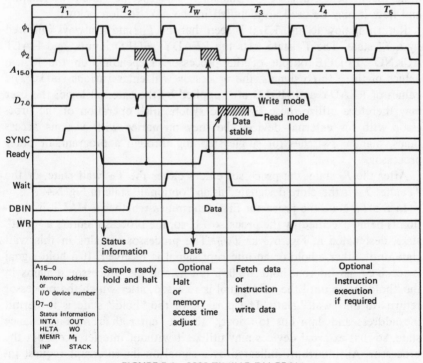

FIGURE 5.4 8080 TIMING DIAGRAM.

clock is considerably wider than that of the ϕ_1 clock. Furthermore, a close inspection will also show that the pulses are not symmetrical: the leading edge of ϕ_2 is closer to the trailing edge of ϕ_1 than the leading edge of ϕ_1 is to the trailing edge of ϕ_2. The exact electrical specifications for the microprocessor will be presented later in the section on Electrical Specifications, but the peculiar clock cycles used in the 8080 microprocessor should be brought to the user's attention also in connection with the instruction timing cycle.

During the T_1 cycle the contents of the program counter register are placed on the address bus $(A_0\!-\!A_{15})$. Since the program counter contains the address of the next instruction, it now becomes the task of the external logic to locate that instruction and make it available to the processor at a later state.

After the leading edge of the ϕ_2 pulse in the T_1 state, a synchronization signal is sent out on the SYNC line. This synchronization signal can be used by the designer to activate external circuits to perform the required memory input and output tasks. Status information is also outputted on the data bus $(D_0 - D_7)$ so that the external logic may definitively determine the present status of the machine. The specific status information and how it may be used are detailed in the next section below.

Returning now to Fig. 5.3, it is seen that the T_1 state is always followed by a T_2 state. The T_2 state tests the READY, HOLD inputs, and HALT ACKNOWLEDGE output of the processor. Depending on the logical values of these three signals, the processor will enter various states. The values of READY and HOLD are supplied by the external logic; the user may therefore utilize these signals to synchronize operation of the processor with his external devices, be they memories with various access times, manual switches for single stepping through a program, or other processors.

After the T_2 state, the processor enters either the T_W wait state, or the T_3 state; T_W is therefore designated as an "optional" state in Fig. 5.4.

In the T_W state the processor first determines whether a HALT instruction is being executed by the processor. If so, the processor enters a "wait" state, designated in Fig. 5.3 as T_{WH}. The processor remains in this wait state until either a hold or an interrupt signal is received. If a hold signal is received, an internal hold flip-flop is set, and the processor remains in the "hold" state until the hold signal is released, after which the processor returns to the "wait" state. The purpose of the "hold" state is to permit the address and data bus to "float," that is, enter their high-impedance state, so that external devices may utilize it without interference from the processor. An interrupt, indicated by a signal on the interrupt request input, takes the processor out of the "wait" state to begin execution of the interrupt routine.

If the HALT instruction is not being executed by the processor, the processor enters the "wait" state designated by T_W in Fig. 5.3. The processor remains in this T_W state until the ready line goes high, indicating that valid data are available for the processor on the data bus. If no HOLD signal is received, the processor proceeds to the T_3 state.

The T_3 state enables the data available on the data bus to be transferred into the instruction register. During the first *machine cycle*, such as after a new instruction has been fetched in the T_3 state, the processor proceeds to the T_4 state for execution of the instruction.

The instruction in the instruction register is decoded and execution begins during the T_4 state. A determination is made of how many states or machine cycles are needed to execute the instruction, and appropriate timing and synchronization signals generated.

For example, the simple ADD B instruction ("add the contents of register B to the accumulator") requires only four clock cycles (see Fig. 5.2). After execution of the instruction in the T_4 state of the first machine cycle, the processor returns to the T_1 state of a new machine cycle to begin execution of a new instruction. In other words, for this instruction there is no T_5 state during the machine cycle.

More complex instructions, such as memory reference instructions, may require the T_5 state, as well as one or two more additional machine cycles for execution of the single instruction.

An illustration of the manner in which instructions are executed over several machine cycles may be made with reference to Fig. 5.5. Figure 5.5 is a representation of the input instruction IN, $<B_2>$, where B_2 is the second byte of the instruction. The IN instruction is executed over 3 machine cycles or 10 clock cycles of T-states.

In the first machine cycle (M_1) there are four states, T_1, T_2, T_3, and T_4. Fig. 5.5 gives the position of the levels of the various pins of the 8080, the address pins $(A_{15} - A_0)$, the data pins $(D_7 - D_0)$, and SYNC, DBIN, READY, WAIT, and $\overline{WR}$. The bottom of the figure indicates the code that is sent out over the data pins which indicates the type of machine cycle being executed. The M_1 cycle for a new instruction is represented by a 10100010 signal which is put out on the data bus, designating an "instruction fetch," as shown in the first data column of the Status Word Chart in Fig. 5.6.

In the second machine cycle (M_2) there are three states, T_1, T_2, T_3. Byte two of the instruction, $<B_2>$, is read.

In the third and last machine cycle (M_3), there are also three states,

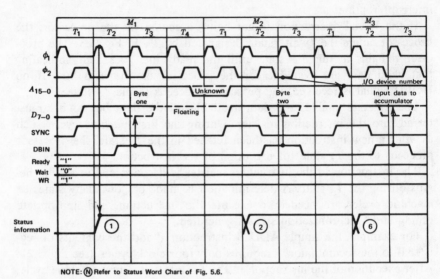

NOTE: ⓃRefer to Status Word Chart of Fig. 5.6.

FIGURE 5.5 8080 "IN" INSTRUCTION CYCLE.

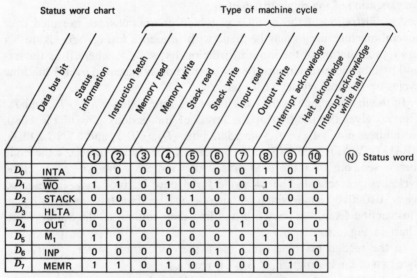

		①	②	③	④	⑤	⑥	⑦	⑧	⑨	⑩	Ⓝ Status word
D_0	INTA	0	0	0	0	0	0	0	1	0	1	
D_1	$\overline{WO}$	1	1	0	1	0	1	0	1	1	0	
D_2	STACK	0	0	0	1	1	0	0	0	0	0	
D_3	HLTA	0	0	0	0	0	0	0	0	1	1	
D_4	OUT	0	0	0	0	0	0	1	0	0	0	
D_5	M_1	1	0	0	0	0	0	0	1	0	1	
D_6	INP	0	0	0	0	0	1	0	0	0	0	
D_7	MEMR	1	1	0	1	0	0	0	0	1	0	

FIGURE 5.6 STATUS DECODING CHART.

T_1, T_2, and T_3. The Status Word Chart indicates that an input read operation takes place, and data from the designated I/O device are inputed to the accumulator.

Status Decoding

To synchronize the operation of the 8080 with respect to external logic devices, it is necessary to determine and provide current operational status operation of the 8080 during each machine cycle. As pointed out above, such status information is provided on the data bus (pins $D_0 - D_7$) during the T_1 state. It is the task of the system designer to latch these data during the T_1 state so that they may be utilized by other devices in the system.

Microcomputer systems typically use a decoder or I/O port latch having a number of controlled flip-flops, or a more sophisticated system controller device or chip. The clock signals and synchronization pulses from the microprocessor are decoded to specify the T_1 cycle, producing a signal to the latch to store the data appearing on the data bus.

Fig. 5.7 shows a typical status latching arrangement. This particular example uses an Intel 8212 latch which is attached to the data bus. The control signals it receives are from the SYNC output of the 8080, as well as from the clock generator. Fig. 5.8 is the internal logic diagram of the 8212 to show in greater detail the D-flip-flops and control circuitry found in the chip.

The information provided on the data bus during the T_1 state must be decoded and interpreted so that a single discrete indication may be made that the processor is in a given state and operational status. The interpretation of the type of machine cycle being executed may be made with the aid of the chart in Fig. 5.6 based on the output of the 8212.

ELECTRICAL SPECIFICATION

The electrical specification of a microprocessor is not a factor in a microcomputer system that can be casually overlooked. Clock cycles and timing differences are essential for the proper operation and synchronization of a logic device, and even slight deviations throughout the system could create discrepancies which could be extremely difficult to detect and isolate.

The specification for the clock period and associated cycles is shown in

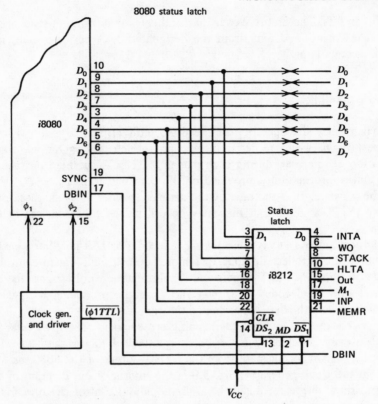

FIGURE 5.7   8080 STATUS LATCHING BLOCK DIAGRAM.

Fig. 5.9. The specified clock period of 0.48 to 2.0 microseconds, or from 500 kilohertz to 2 megahertz, deserves some comment. This range is meant to define an operating range at which the 8080 should be driven. The device is, of course, functionally operable at the maximum and higher clock speeds. Operation at such speeds, however, does affect internal components in the 8080, and extended operation may lead to shorter life and decreased device reliability.

Fig. 5.9a lists the specification of the clock cycle, while Fig. 5.9b represents the clock waveform itself.

Some microcomputer systems take advantage of the wide operating range of clock speeds to adapt the system to different operating circumstances. If, for example, the system is used in an environment where it is possible that the ambient temperature may become relatively high for an interval of time, means may be provided for switching the clock speed

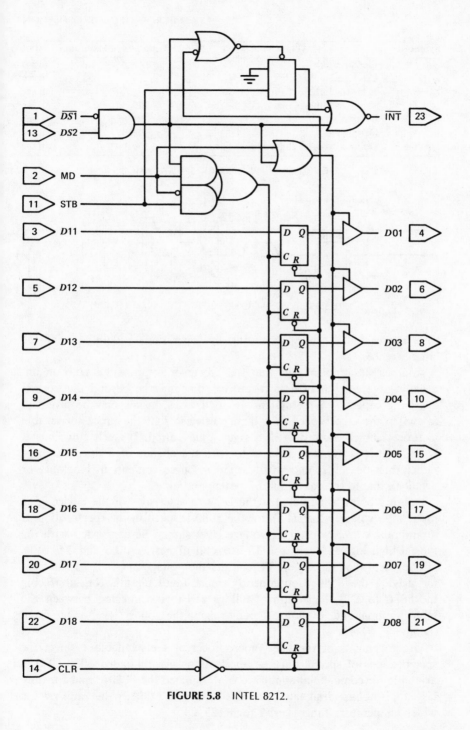

FIGURE 5.8 INTEL 8212.

Symbol	Parameter	Minimum	Maximum	Unit
t_{CY}[3]	Clock period	0.48	2.0	μ sec
t_r, t_f	Clock rise and fall time	5	50	n sec
$t_{\emptyset 1}$	ϕ_1 pulsewidth	60		n sec
$t_{\emptyset 2}$	ϕ_2 pulsewidth	220		n sec
t_{D1}	Delay ϕ_1 to ϕ_2	0		n sec
t_{D2}	Delay ϕ_2 to ϕ_1	70		n sec
t_{D3}	Delay ϕ_1 to ϕ_2 leading edges	130		n sec

FIGURE 5.9A   8080 CLOCK SPECIFICATION.

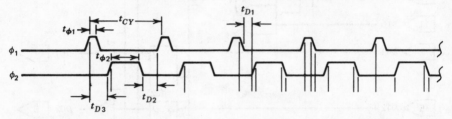

FIGURE 5.9B   8080 CLOCK SPECIFICATION WAVEFORM.

to a slower rate, thereby increasing the operating reliability under the circumstances.

Another situation may be that the processor is presented with an unusually large amount of data to process that may be beyond the normal operating capacity of the system. In such cases, means may be provided to switch the clock speed to a higher rate, so that the processor is able to process much more data in a given time period. In such situations it is felt that it is more reasonable to take the chance of a device failing, rather than be confronted with certain resource contention, blocking, or deadlock due to the saturation of system resources.

Another point to be noted is the DC characteristics of the device. The input high voltage (logical-1) for the 8080 is listed in the specification as a minimum of 3.3 volts. This voltage level should be contrasted with the typical high logical levels in a TTL circuit of between 2.5 and 3.5 volts. It is evident that for some TTL circuits the voltage may not be sufficient for driving the 8080. Consequently, most input circuits for interfacing the 8080 to TTL logic utilize pull-up resistors connected between the input terminal and +5 volts, thereby raising the voltage level of the input signal.

Other versions of the 8080 microprocessor are available to meet the specifications of special purpose applications. An upgraded 8080 CPU is available for commercial applications, designated the 8080A, and for military applications, designated the M8080A. The M8080A operates over a wider temperature range (-55 to $+125°C$).

For high-speed processing requirements, the 8080 is also available in two models designated 8080A-1 and 8080A-2. The 8080A-1 operates at a cycle time of 1.5 microseconds, and the 8080A-2 at 1.3 microseconds.

INTERFACES

The 8080 must be interfaced with the rest of the microcomputer system through appropriate latches and decoding logic. The purpose of such interface logic is to synchronize operation of the microprocessor with the rest of the system. Latches are provided so that in the particular time interval when the microprocessor requests data, they are available, and when the microprocessor is ready to output data, they may be outputted and stored for later system use.

The simple status latching arrangement shown in Fig. 5.7 is merely one such way to achieve a suitable interface. Another method, using a single-chip System Controller and Bus Driver, is shown in Fig. 5.10.

Another important aspect of interfacing is the driving capability ("fan-out") of the output stage of the microprocessor. The 8080 is an MOS de-

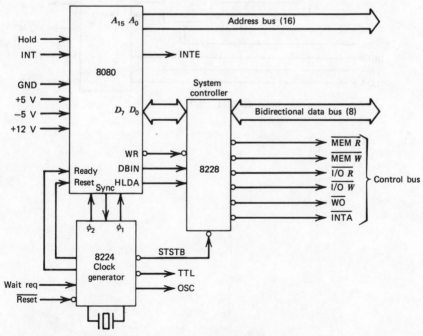

FIGURE 5.10   8228 SYSTEM CONTROLLER INTERFACE.

vice, and accordingly has a very limited driving capacity. It may be safely stated that the driving capacity is *one* TTL load. Since most systems require greater driving capabilities, it is ncessary to provide an interface between the microprocessor output and the TTL logic in the remainder of the system. One technique is to use the Bus Driver as shown in Fig. 5.11.

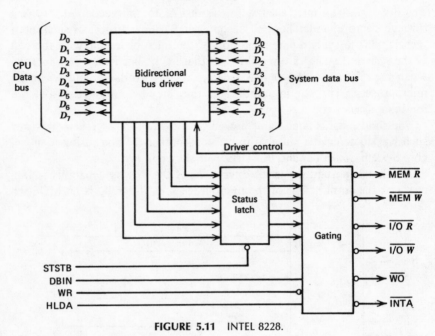

FIGURE 5.11   INTEL 8228.

CHAPTER SIX
MICROPROCESSOR
PROGRAMMING

Since one of the most important advantages of a microprocessor over other forms of digital logic is the ability to replace hardware by software, it is evident that microprocessor programmer should be an important topic in microcomputer system design.

Microprocessor programming is one of the first tasks of the systems designer in constructing a microcomputer system. As we have suggested in Chapter 2, we assume that the designer would most likely begin his initial development work on a commercially available microprocessor development system equipped with an assembler. The system designer must then write a program for execution on his development system that corresponds to the system function and operation that he requires. This initial task can be elaborated into the following elements:

> system definition
> functional flow-charting
> program flow-charting
> coding
> testing and debugging

SYSTEM DEFINITION

Before tackling the programming task per se, the designer must explicitly specify the system elements to be incorporated into the microcomputer system. Such a system definition or specification must at least include the following elements:

> I/O specification
> system memory
> arithmetic and logical operations
> control functions

I/O Specification

The varieties of I/O devices were detailed in Chapter 2 from the point of view of hardware. In terms of programming, the system designer must realize that each device has its own particular formats and coding structure which must be synchronized and decoded for compatibility with the microcomputer system.

In applications where a wide variety of characters are utilized, two standard codes are utilized: ASCII and EBCDIC. The definition and specification of these two important codes are given in Fig. 6.1 and 6.2

In communications applications data must be more than coded. They must be formated into particular groups so that an external terminal or communications device knows when data are being transmitted and when a message begins or ends. Such formating is known as "data link control" or "line protocol." There is at present no data link control standard, although the American National Standards Institute (ANSI) is in the process of developing one for the United States, called the Advanced Data Communications Control Procedure (ADCCP). The International Standards Organization (ISO) is also actively working toward the definition of an international standard.

In the meantime manufacturers are shipping communications products and have developed their own "standards." Examples of such standard protocols are IBM's Synchronous Data Link Control (SDLC), and Digital Equipment Corporation's Digital Data Communications Message Protocol (DDCMP). IC chips are already under development to handle such protocols, or to convert messages in one protocol to a message in another protocol. An example of how a microcomputer may be programmed to handle a communications protocol will be presented in Chapter 9, in connection with a packet communications application.

Another important factor that must be considered by the designer is that of timing relationships between the microprocessor and the peripherals. The speed at which the external peripherals and sensor and control devices operate is important not only in the initial selection of the microprocessor but also in the programming of the microprocessor. For peripherals operating at data transfer rates considerably slower than that of the microprocessor, there is no problem. However, if one is using fairly sophisticated peripherals a critical design problem may arise in synchronizing the data transfer rate of the peripheral with that of the processor.

One of the most common peripherals that presents such a critical design problem is the floppy disk.

Floppy Disk Specification.   The floppy disk, or "diskette," is a Mylar

$b_3b_2b_1b_0$	ASCII character set (7-bit code) [a]			$b_6b_5b_4$				
	000	001	010	011	100	101	110	111
0000	NUL	DLE	SP	0	'	P	@	p
0001	SOH	DC1	1	1	A	Q	a	g
0010	STX	DC2	"	2	B	R	b	r
0011	ETX	DC3	#	3	C	S	c	s
0100	EOT	DC4	$	4	D	T	d	t
0101	ENQ	NAK	%	5	E	U	e	u
0110	ACK	SYN	&	6	F	V	f	v
0111	BEL	ETB	'	7	G	W	g	w
1000	BS	CAN	(	8	H	X	h	x
1001	HT	EM	)	9	I	Y	i	y
1010	LF	SUB	*	:	J	Z	j	z
1011	VT	ESC	+	;	K	[	k	{
1100	FF	S	,	<	L	\	l	:
1101	CR	GS	–	=	M	]	m	}
1110	SO	RS	•	>	N	↑	n	~
1111	SI	US	/	?	O	↓	o	DEL

[a] Control characters:

NULL	—Null/idle	DLE	—Data link escape (CC)
SOH	—Start of heading (CC)	DC1	
STX	—Start of text (CC)	DC2	—Device controls
ETX	—End of text (CC)	DC3	
EOT	—End of transmission (CC)	DC4	—Device control (stop)
ENQ	—Enquiry (CC)	NAK	—Negative acknowledge (CC)
ACK	—Acknowledge (CC)	SYN	—Synchronous idle CC
BEL	—Audible or attention signal	ETB	—End of transmission block (CC)
BS	—Backspace (FE)		
HT	—Horizontal tabulation (punch card skip) (FE)	C	—Cancel
		EM	—End of medium
LF	—Line feed (FE)	SS	—Start of special sequence
VT	—Vertical tabulation (FE)	ESC	—Escape
FF	—Form feed (FE)	FS	—File separator (IS)
CR	—Carriage return (FE)	GS	—Group separator (IS)
SO	—Shift out	RS	—Record separator (IS)
SI	—Shift in	US	—Unit separator (IS)
		DEL	—Delete

Note: b_i represents the ith bit position.

FIGURE 6.1 ASCII CODE.

EBCDIC Character Set

Bit positions → b_7b_6

b_5b_4 —00— —01— —10— —11—

$b_3b_2b_1b_0$	00	01	10	11	00	01	10	11	00	01	10	11	00	01	10	11
0000	NULL				SP	8	−									0
0001							/		a	j			A	J		1
0010									b	k	s		B	K	S	2
0011									c	l	t		C	L	T	3
0100	PF	RES	BYP	PN					d	m	u		D	M	U	4
0101	HT	NL	LF	RC					e	n	v		E	N	V	5
0110	LC	BS	EOB	UC					f	o	w		F	O	W	6
0111	DEL	IL	PR	EOT					g	p	x		G	P	X	7
1000									h	q	y		H	Q	Y	8
1001									i	r	z		I	R	Z	9
1010		SM			¢	!										
1011					.	$	,	#								
1100					<	*	%	@								
1101					(	)	—	'								
1110					+	;	>	=								
1111							?	"								

Control characters:

NULL	— All zero—bits	BS	— Backspace	PN	— Punch on
PF	— Punch off	IL	— Idle	RS	— Reader stop
HT	— Horizontal tab	BYP	— Bypass	UC	— Upper case
LC	— Lower case	LF	— Line feed	EOT	— End of transmission
DEL	— Delete	EOB	— End of block	SM	— Set mode
RES	— Restore	PR	— Prefix	SP	— Space
NL	— New line				

Chart is read by order of significance as designated by "Bit positions,"i.e., b_7 is 2^7 bit, b_6 is 2^6 bit . . . etc.

FIGURE 6.2   EBCDIC CODE.

disk 0.005 inch thick, 7.8 inches in diameter, with a 1.5-inch hole in the center. It is coated with oxide to form a magnetic recording surface and is packaged in a flexible plastic envelope to protect the oxide layer. In actual use, the diskette and plastic envelope are inserted into the drive, and the read/write head of the drive is fitted into a slot on one edge of the envelope, thereby coming into contact with the oxide layer.

The floppy disk was originally developed by IBM as a means for storing the control program for a large disk controller. Later, it was introduced as part of the IBM 3740 key-to-disk data entry system. The use of floppy disks as part of data entry systems was widely imitated by other manufacturers, and their use gradually spread to other applications.

The IBM recording format standard has also been adopted by many of the manufacturers of floppy disks. The IBM format divides the disk into 77 tracks, as shown in Fig. 6.3*a*. Each track consists of 26 sections (Fig. 6.3*b*). Each section is in turn consists of 128 bytes, which includes a

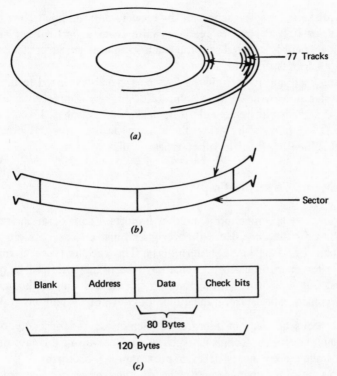

77 Tracks

(a)

Sector

(b)

Blank	Address	Data	Check bits

80 Bytes

120 Bytes

(c)

FIGURE 6.3 FLOPPY DISK FORMAT.

blank field, an address field, a data field, and a check bit field (Fig. 6.3c).
Consequently, each diskette has about 243,000 bytes.

The particular advantage of the flexible or "floppy" disk over the rigid
disk is that they are relatively simple to manufacture, since they consist
simply of a magnetic oxide coating on a Mylar disk. The low cost of such
data storage facilities is particularly suitable in the low-cost microcomputer
environment.

The floppy disk presents a number of critical timing and programming
issues which must be considered by the system designer. With the disk
rotating at 360 rpm (the IBM standard format), an 8-bit byte will be
ready for processing every 32 microseconds. Such timing considerations
may be important if the system has a considerable overhead in system
programming.

Because of the importance of the diskette to microcomputer systems, it
is worthwhile to mention another peripheral product which is now under
development: the multiple diskette file. Because of the thinness of diskettes, a large number of them may be stacked in a small space. Such

stacked diskettes may be separated by spacers and mounted on a rotating shaft. When it is desired to read or write from a particular diskette, a wedging element is inserted into the stack so that magnetic contact is made with the selected disk surface.

Moving-head and fixed rigid-disk systems are also utilized in microcomputer systems. Moving-head systems offer higher storage capacities and may be designed with removable disk packs or cartridges. Fixed-head systems (i.e., nonremovable disks) have faster access time and greater mechanical reliability than do other types of disk systems.

System Memory Specification

System memory specification is another important consideration for microprocessor programming. Here the designer must choose between various technological and packaging alternatives. The various types of memories available for microprocessor systems have been characterized in previous chapters, but it is worthwhile pointing out here some of the more important considerations from the point of view of system programming:

system consequences of hierarchial memories: the necessity of using more than one storage technique, such as for back-up in the case of power failure, immediately necessitates a programming problem.

memory resource management: the dividing of workspace among the various available memories in the system, a task most suitably performed by software.

utilization of memory, particularly read-only memory, for test and diagnotic routines.

architecturally structuring the system around memory microcode so as to provide system reconfigurability merely by changing one or two read-only memory chips.

The considerations noted above are derived from large-scale computer concepts but apply equally as well to microprocessor systems. The fact that such concepts are important in larger systems only reinforces their significance for microprocessor implementations. All of these considerations must be evaluated by the designer, and appropriate implementations of corresponding memory design features must be made in both hardware and software.

Arithmetic and Logical Operations

The nature of the arithmetic and logical operations to be performed are a key element in the microprocessor programming task. Various types of instructions are performed by all processors in one way or another: binary and decimal arithmetic, logical functions, bit manipulation functions (shift, rotate), and memory management.

Some processors perform certain of these functions faster than others. In performing the system definition task, the designer should carefully consider the *types* of instructions, as well as their *frequency*, that are likely to appear in the final system program. With this information, the designer may make several important determinations:

the choice of microprocessor
system hardware architecture
system software structure

If, for example, the intended application deals with extensive mathematical calculations (i.e., uses decimal arithmetic), the designer would make the availability of decimal arithmetic instructions an important criterion in selecting the microprocessor. The system hardware architecture could also be decimal oriented, such as by supplying a decimal point on the keyboard and displays. And the system software structure would be adapted to handle decimal calculations routinely. This is in fact how pocket scientific calculators are designed.

The designer has three basic means for implementing given arithmetic or logical functions in a microcomputer system:

microprocessor instructions
microprogramming
hardwired logic

The essential difference between these approaches is speed. For the average system, the implementation of arithmetical or logical functions through microprocessor instructions is usually sufficient. However, for some applications, such as real time or signal processing applications, speed may be critical. Although the complexity of the task may not require the capabilities of a minicomputer, microprocessors may not operate at sufficient rates to satisfy all possible input conditions. In such cases, one or both of the noted implementations above may be utilized.

Microprogramming.   Microprogramming is a computer design technique for providing a programmable control circuit for controlling the operation of a digital computer. Although microprogramming was first proposed by Dr. M. V. Wilkes in 1951, it was not until the development of suitable read-only memories that it was introduced on any widespread commercial scale.

Microprogramming replaces a long sequence of microprocessor instructions by a single microprogram instruction. For example, instead of a sequence of instructions for performing an integer "multiply" operation, the user may specify that "multiply" is to be a new microprogram instruction. This specification of a new instruction is made to the microprocessor manufacturer, so that a custom designed CROM (control and read-only memory), or its equivalent, may be provided for the system.

The customized microprogram memory contains a sequence of *microinstructions* which correspond to the single microprogram instruction. These microinstructions perform the operations of multiplication in the microprocessor much more efficiently than a series of microprocessor instructions. Since the microinstructions are executed on the basis of internal microinstruction cycle times, a significant time advantage over regular microprocessor programming is achieved.

In addition to speed, the other advantage is that the coding may take place in a user-defined instruction set. For long programs, or those utilizing complex operations and functions, microprogramming considerably simplifies the programming task.

The basic design of a microprogrammable computer is shown in Fig. 6.4. The microprogram instructions are applied to a decoder, which specifies a memory location in the read-only memory where the particular sequence of microinstructions corresponding to that microprogram instruction begins. The controller then indicates the succeeding memory locations of further microinstructions, until the microprogram instruction execution is complete. Control is then returned to the next machine instruction.

A more sophisticated treatment of microprogramming will also refer to the structure of the microinstructions themselves as a particular combination of serial and parallel operations. These two operational modes are referred to as "vertical" and "horizontal" microprogramming, respectively. A more detailed explanation of these concepts, and their applica-

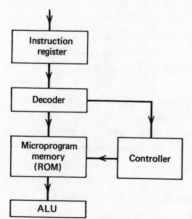

FIGURE 6.4 MICROPROGRAMMING SYSTEM.

tion, can be found in the books on microprogramming noted in the bibliography.

Hardwired Logic. Hardwired logic should not be automatically dismissed from consideration in planning a microcomputer system. In situations where time is a critical factor, and where function or algorithm is being frequently executed, a hardwired logic implementation of that function external to the microprocessor would be able to save considerable time at the cost of only a few additional circuits. Some applications making heavy use of multiplication, for example, have found that the use of an external digital multiplier implemented in hardware would perform a 16-bit multiplication over 25 times as fast as using the microprocessor. If the application was a real-time one, such as a digital filter, such considerations could be of critical importance.

Control Functions

In addition to the normal arithmetical and logical input and output operations, many applications require that the processor perform certain purely supervisory or control functions. These functions include:

operating facility management
system administration
network control
program and job control
data management

Although these functions may seem sophisticated for a microprocessor system, they are important for many applications. Just like the specification of arithmetic or logical operations, the specification of the control operations is determinative in the choice of microprocessor, as well as the hardware and software structure of the system.

Operating facility management is concerned with management of the system hardware facilities, including power supplies, displays, and peripherals. Conditions such as power-on and power-off may be detected and responded to.

System administration is concerned with the control and scheduling of system resources, including memory, the processor, buses, and I/O devices. If several users have access to the system, an accounting function may also be performed.

Network control is concerned with the management of remote terminals or of a communications link. Control tasks, such as polling and interrupt handling, and communications protocol handling are examples of network control functions.

Program and job control are concerned with the ability of the processor to manage the system job flow and to perform program monitoring and control functions.

Data management is concerned with the formation and organization of data structures and files.

FUNCTIONAL FLOW CHARTING

While the System Definition task breaks the microprocessor system into hardware component elements, the Functional Flow Charting task breaks the system into software component elements. These software components or modules represent different discrete operations to be performed by the different hardware component elements of the system.

The different operations are performed in a predetermined sequence to accomplish an overall desired result. This sequence of operations is represented by a connected series of modules or boxes. Each of the modules represents a particular group of operations. When that group of operations. is completed, a connecting line leads to another module, whose group of operations is in turn executed. The resulting representation of operations is called a flowchart.

There are a number of different types of flow charts depending on the detail of specification of the modules. In actual practice, the system designer first draws the broadest possible flowchart, and then gradually refines in as he specifies the system in more detail. The different type of modules that many be represented in a flowchart are:

macros
procedures
functions
routines

A *macro* is defined as a supervisory service command that generally refers to an operation that is executed external to the processor, for example, "read input tape."

A *procedure* is a group of machine operations that are closely related by reason of operating on the same data, or directed at achieving a particular result, for example, "find Fourier transform."

A *function* is a particular machine operation that may be part of a broader overall procedure, for example, "multiply by sin A."

A *routine* is a specialized machine procedure for performing a specific calculation, such as "calculate sin A."

As an example of a functional flow chart, we consider a program to test or poll a peripheral device. Fig. 6.5 illustrates a functional flow chart for performing a simple polling function, labelling the data obtained, and storing it in memory. Since the program is relatively simple, the modules of the functional flow chart represent machine functions or operations, rather than more general macro statements.

The program illustrated in the flow chart of Fig. 6.5 is also a good example of a benchmark program.

Benchmark Programs

A benchmark program is a simple program or routine used to compare the performance of different processors. Since different processors utilize different instruction sets, such programs are typically specified by means of a functional flow chart.

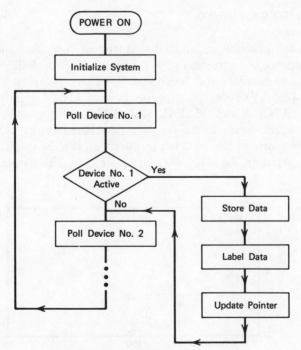

FIGURE 6.5 FUNCTIONAL FLOW CHART.

From the functional flow chart, experienced programmers in the language of the processor being tested code and run the program. Two of the key parameters that are considered in comparing performance are:

number of memory bytes occupied by the program
speed of execution of the program

The relative importance of each of these parameters depend on the application, and a benchmark program establishes a quantitative measure for making a comparison. Of course, a complex program or operational application contains numerous routines, and conclusive information cannot be drawn from merely one or two sample benchmarks.

Fig. 6.6 is an example of the presentation of the result of a benchmark test using the sample program represented by the flow chart in Fig. 6.5. Although the results shown reflect an actual test of various commercially available microprocessors, the identification of the specific products is omitted to avoid prejudicing any particular product by presenting the data on only one benchmark.

PROGRAM FLOW CHARTING

The program flowchart expands the functional flowchart and lists the specific sequence of instruction steps for performing the desired operation. Whereas, for example, the functional flowchart provides a command "INITIALIZE SYSTEM," a program flowchart may specify "CLEAR ACCUMULATOR," and "CLEAR REGISTER B."

The statements made in the program flowchart more specifically refer to the architecture of the machine in question; that is, specific reference is made to registers, flags, or other characteristics. The translation of the

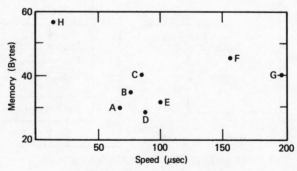

FIGURE 6.6   BENCHMARK RESULTS.

program flowchart to the assembly language code is therefore direct, and is almost on a one-to-one basis. For example, the programmer is able to code the instruction to "CLEAR ACCUMULATOR" in only one instruction, by using an "exclusive or" operation, if the processor includes such an instruction. In the Intel 8080 instruction set and assembly language, such an instruction is written "XRA." An exclusive or of the accumulator, or any register for that matter, with itself gives zero. For more complex commands, or for processors with a limited instruction set, more than one assembly language instruction may be necessary to represent one line of the program flowchart.

The process of translating the program flowchart into assembly language is known as coding, and will be analyzed in more detail in the following section.

CODING

Coding is defined as translating the sequence of steps presented in the program flow chart as a sequence of instructions for execution by the processor. The system designer has a choice in deciding to code in either a high level language or to use the assembly language provided with the processor. This choice is dependent on at least the following factors:

the availability of programmers experienced in assembly language and higher level language programming.

the length and complexity of the system program.

the criticalness of program size and execution speed.

the amount of time available for program development.

The task of coding has been greatly simplified by the availability of microprocessor development systems with a large number of software aids. These development systems and software aids are discussed in the next chapter.

Coding essentially consists of selecting the appropriate operator and operand from the instruction set of the processor for performing the statement required in the program flow chart. An assembly language coded statement consists of the following fields:

LABEL   OPERATOR   OPERAND   REMARKS

The LABEL field specifies a particular memory location for locating the succeeding instruction (OPERATOR and OPERAND). The LABEL field is chosen at the option of the user and is merely a symbolic designation of that memory location. If the program must make reference to a particular instruction or point in the program, such as for a jump instruction, the programmer designates that instruction or program point by its LABEL.

The OPERATOR field specifies the mnemonic for the machine instruction to be executed. Depending on the particular microprocessor, the OPERATOR may also specify the type of addressing mode, or other value or condition that will affect the subsequent execution of the instruction.

The OPERAND field specifies the data or address of the data which are to be operated on by the instruction in the OPERATOR field.

The REMARKS field is provided as a convenience to the programmer and is disregarded in compilation of the machine instructions.

At the coding level, the system designer or programmer must pay particular attention to the manner in which data are represented in the computer. This is especially true in the case of signed numbers. It would be suitable to review the various techniques for representing signed numbers in a computer at this point.

Digital Representation of Signed Numbers

Computers operate with fixed point numbers, that is, integers. In order to represent signed or floating point (i.e., nonintegral) numbers a special technique must be used in the computer itself. The representation of signed numbers is discussed below, while floating point arithmetic is discussed in the programming section.

There are three methods for representing signed number in a computer:

signed magnitude
1's complement
2's complement

The signed magnitude representation is the simplest. Suppose a word in a given computer is k bits long. The registers are also assumed to be k bits long. In the signed magnitude representation the leftmost bit of the word indicates the sign of the number in that register. A 0-bit in the leftmost bit position of the register is designated as representing a positive integer, while a 1-bit in the leftmost bit of the register represents a negative integer. The remaining k-1 bits in the register represent the magnitude of the number itself.

One's or 2's complement representation employs variations of the number following the sign bit depending on whether the number is positive or negative. Such variations are utilized to simplify various arithmethic calculations when using negative numbers in the computer.

The 1's complement method represents a positive integer in the same manner as the signed magnitude representation: a sign bit followed by the magnitude of the integer. A negative number is represented by taking a 1-bit in the leftmost bit position and by taking the complement (i.e., "1's complement") of the remaining k-1 bits representing the magnitude of the stored number.

The 2's complement method represents a positive integer in the same manner as a signed magnitude representation. A negative number is represented by taking 1 for the leftmost bit position, and $1 - X$ for the remaining $k - 1$ bits, where X represents the magnitude of the number.

A few examples would be useful here. Consider first binary number representations and consider a 4-bit word for simplicity. The positive integer 3 has the following representations:

signed magnitude   0011
1's complement   0011
2's complement   0011

The difference is found in the representation of the negative integer −3:

signed magnitude   1011
1's complement   1100
2's complement   1101

Since it is impractical to write out 1's and 0's to refer to addresses and data in the computer, the octal or hexadecimal number system is used, since they are based on powers of 2. Compilers for the assembly language of many microprocessors are written so that the programmer may code his addresses and data in octal notation, and the computer automatically converts it into binary for the computer.

Coding Examples

We consider a few simple programs as examples of microprocessor instruction coding. The instruction set and assembly language illustrated is that of the Intel 8080 presented in Fig. 5.2.

Arithmetic Operations. As an example of a simple arithmetic operation, we consider the evaluation of the arithmetic expression

$$R = S + T - U$$

where S, T, and U are integers. There are, of course, a number of different ways of performing even this simple calculation with a microprocessor, and the program listed below is merely an example of one such way.

We use the accumulator, which is designated by 111, in the calculation:

> MVI 111
> S   (load the accumulator with S)
> ADI
> T   (add T to the accumulator)
> SUI
> U   (subtract U from the accumulator)

The quantity remaining in the accumulator is the result R. It must also be remembered that the number in the accumulator is in 2's complement representation.

Looping Operations. The use of a looping operation to perform an iterative calculation is one of the most useful features in programming. The looping operation program presented below also illustrates the use of the LABEL field. The particular program below performs a looping operation by counting down from a predetermined number set in a register, and testing during each loop to determine if the contents of the register is zero. If the indexed number in the register is not zero, the program returns to the instruction designated by the label LOOP.

> ```
>           LXI D
>           N                (load register D with the value N)
> LOOP      . . . .
>           . . . .
>           . . . .          (instructions to be iterated)
>           DCR D            (decrement the loop counter by 1)
>           JNZ LOOP         (return to LOOP if D register not zero)
>           . . . .          (next instruction)
> ```

In the example above register D served as the loop counter, but any other register could have been used as well. Once the register D has been decremented to zero, and the JNZ instruction detects the zero, the looping operation will be stopped, and the program counter (PC) will be set to execute the next instruction, as noted in the description of the JNZ instruction in Fig. 5.2.

The technique of programming and assembly language coding for a microprocessor is highly dependent on the architecture and instruction set of the microprocessor. Reference is therefore made to the specific programming manuals for various microprocessors noted in the Bibliography for more detailed and practical coding examples.

TESTING AND DEBUGGING

Testing and debugging is the final and most critical step in microprocessor programming and may be considered as part of the reliability design phase of the microcomputer system. In this context, reliability design consists of the following elements:

testing of microcomputer software
testing of microcomputer hardware/software design
testing of system, including peripherals
design of field diagnostic routines
design of field modification techniques
development of product expandability

Microcomputer software is most easily tested on the system in which it was developed—either the development systems or the large-scale computer. The purpose of software testing is to identify and correct the logical or software-related program bugs before the software is introduced into the new hardware environment. Since the software of a microcomputer system is usually loaded on a ROM, it should be thoroughly tested before the ROMs are programmed.

The programmed ROMs are then loaded into the system and a system checkout of both hardware and software is made. The critical issues here are that of timing and synchronization between the processor and the other logic elements.

A checkout of the peripherals is made next. These are the operating elements, the sensors, storage facilities, and actuators that provide the raw data and transmit the control response of the systems. Again, timing and synchronization between fast and slow peripherals and the processor are the key factors to be resolved in the system program.

As with any piece of sophisticated electronic equipment, the provision for field maintenance is important for ensuring product reliability. Diagnostic software may be provided on ROMs which may be plugged into the system in the field in the place of the ROM containing the usual system control program. This diagnostic software should check operation of the hardware elements of the equipment, and provided suitable error dection messages should an anomality be encountered.

The possibility of field modification and product expandability must also be planned for as part of the software reliability design. System control programs and even hardware functions may be modified during the product's lifetime to accommodate new applications or environments. Suitable provisions must be made both in hardware and software to accommodate different, perhaps larger, system control programs, or user programs.

CHAPTER SEVEN
MICROPROCESSOR
DEVELOPMENT SYSTEMS

Microprocessor manufacturers, as well as the more realistic potential microprocessor users, have realized that the development of an operable microcomputer system starting from a microprocessor and a few associated parts is a formidible task.

To simplify the problem of hardware and software development, many of the microprocessor manufacturers have "packaged" their product in a number of ways that make the microprocessor more immediately accessible and usable by an inexperienced user. These "packages" take a variety of forms: parts families, ready-to-assemble kits, prewired printed circuit (PC) cards, assembled kits, and development systems.

A parts family, as we noted in Chapter 2, is a set of closely related and compatible IC components, such as a clock driver, microprocessor, RAM chip, ROM chip, and I/O chip, packaged in a box and sold in single quantities at a special price by the manufacturer. A parts family is useful to the experienced designer who already posseses basic microcomputer equipment and who wishes to evaluate a new microprocessor and its associated chips.

A ready-to-assemble kit consists of one or more PC cards and a set of ICs and discrete components for assembly on the PC cards. Once assembled, one has an operative microcomputer. Such kits retail for less than $500, and are consequently of interest for hobby or educational purposes. These kits are also available in the form of factory-assembled systems at slightly higher prices. In the least expensive of such kits, program and data entry takes place by means of toggle switches on the front panel, and data output is represented by lighting miniature lamps according to the output bit pattern. Because of the limited capabilities of such kits, these products are not offered by the microprocessor manufacturers but by independent microcomputer systems companies.

Prewired printed circuit cards, including a microprocessor and related interface ICs, are available from a number of microprocessor manufacturers for those users who already possess basic microcomputer equipment (including RAM and ROM), and wish only to evaluate the processor in their existing equipment.

For those potential users who do not possess basic microcomputer equipment, the microprocessor manufacturers have realized the importance of a "microprocessor development system," including all of the basic hardware and software necessary for the development of a prototype microcomputer system. The introduction of such development systems has greatly simplified the task for the system designer. As we noted in Chapter 1, one of the key advantages of the microprocessor is its capability of replacing cost-recurring random logic hardware with non-cost-recurring software. This advantage, however, becomes less significant when the system designer is confronted with the task of designing a hardware system before he can even begin his software development.

To expedite and simplify the software development, the microprocessor development system includes all of the hardware anticipated in the final system, together with software development aids. The system designer can then initially focus on the more important software capabilities of the microprocessor, and later, after the software has been developed and optimized, he can do the custom hardware design capable of implementing the software system he has developed.

These microprocessor development systems are available from the manufacturers as well as from independent companies at a variety of prices and capabilities.

A typical microprocessor development system includes the following:

microprocessor
random-access memory
read-only memory
clock and power supply
I/O interface (such as to a Teletype)
console (including displays of registers, instruction codes)
panel switches (reset, stop, single step, etc.)
software

In selecting a microprocessor development system, the designer or user must consider a few basic questions:

the complexity of the final system, in hardware and software terms.
the configuration of the final system.
the amount of testing to be done of the system.

A microprocessor development system is intended to simplify the most common hardware and software design problems by providing a suitably standard configuration which may be adapted to particular applications, both in hardware and software terms.

SYSTEM DESIGN USING A DEVELOPMENT SYSTEM

As noted above, the first task of the system designer is to select a development system that is most suitable in terms of complexity, configurations, and testing capabilities relative to the final system.

Development systems are usually constructed on a modular basis, with a number of optional plug-in printed circuit boards that offer expanded memory and I/O capabilities. The number of peripherals and testing modules offered with the development system is another important factor to consider in determining the storage and testing requirements of the eventual prototype system that will be constructed using the development system.

A block diagram of a typical development system is shown in Fig. 1. The various peripheral devices envisioned for the system are connectible to the various I/O ports provided in the system. If such devices are not available at the design stage, then simulator I/O may be provided. In addition, a I/O interface is provided for program development on the system. This particular I/O interface would not be necessary in the final system but is only used here to develop software for the system. Such an I/O interface may be a teletype interface, or interface to a keyboard and CRT terminal so that the user may do on-line programming and editing of the system software, without utilizing the full hardware configuration of the final system.

The particular module shown in Fig. 7.1 is the Digital Equipment Corp. M7341 Processor Module (PM), which is based on the Intel 8008 microprocessor. The Processor Module is a one-board configuration which is designed for modular construction of the development sysem.

A modular development system is the most popular form of system since the user has the option of selecting the particular modules that are most particularly suited for his application. The Digital Equipment Corp. system includes the following modules:

read/write memory module
programmable read-only memory module
external event detection module
monitor/control panel
prewired system backplane

The entire system is connected together by means of the backplane, forming the system as shown in Fig. 7.2.

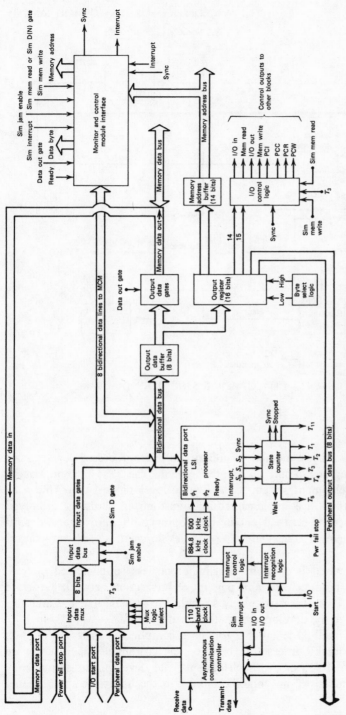

FIGURE 7.1 DEVELOPMENT SYSTEM PROCESSOR MODULE.

145

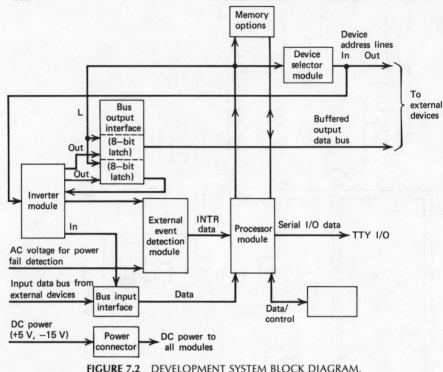

FIGURE 7.2　DEVELOPMENT SYSTEM BLOCK DIAGRAM.

There are two basic methods of utilizing a microprocessor development system in designing a microcomputer system. The first method entails using the development system for software development. Once the software is developed, it is implemented on a customized hardware prototype system. The second method entails developing both hardware and software on the same system and using the development system for control and diagnosis.

The first method is suitable for smaller or less sophisticated systems where there is not a considerable amount of interaction between hardware and software. It is also particularly suitable for systems that are architecturally similar to the development system itself.

The second method is suitable for more complicated systems in which there is considerable interaction between the custom designed hardware and the system software. In such systems, the development system may be linked by means of an "umbilical link" to the hardware system being developed.

SOFTWARE DEVELOPMENT AIDS

With the basic hardware elements of a microcomputer system provided through a development system, the system designer may devote the majority of his attention with software design. As we have noted previously, one of the key advantages of a microprocessor system is its ability to replace hardware components by software. An optimum microprocessor system design is one that optimizes the software and coding.

As we noted in Chapter 6, microprocessor program development is not an easy task. The microprocessor manufacturers have realized this and have developed a number of software development aids for use with their development systems. These aids include:

assemblers
cross-assemblers
higher level languages
editors
loaders
debuggers
simulators
PROM programmers

An *assembler* converts the symbolic code written by the programmer into machine language instructions which are executable by the processor. The assembler converts the symbolic instructions (such as ADD, SUB, etc.) into machine instructions—the 1's and 0's bit pattern. It further converts the labelled machine addresses designated by the programmer into real machine memory locations.

A *cross-assembler* converts the symbolic code written by the programmer into machine language instructions that are executable not by the processor, but by another computer, such as a minicomputer or large scale computer. The point of using a cross-assembler is that execution, testing, and debugging a program is not a simple task on a microprocessor development system. If the input is a Teletype, a paper tape must be punched and loaded into the processor, which is a long, arduous process. The microprocessor system itself may not possess all the facilities to fully analyze each program step, and the detection of critical breakpoints may be difficult to implement. A cross-assembler permits the programmer to design, develop, and refine his program on a larger, more familiar computer. Cross assemblers have been written for minicomputers, and even on large-scale computers by means of time-sharing services.

It is also important to mention the development of *high level languages* for use with development systems. The use of high level languages greatly simplifies the task of the system designer. However, it must be noted that the efficiency of coding in a high level language is considerably poorer than what could be achieved using assembly language. Although the use of high level languages may be acceptable for hobby or instructional purposes, the development of microprocessor systems for commercial applications places much more critical requirements on the software.

At the present time, two high level languages have been developed for microprocessor development systems—PL/M for use with the Intel 8080 development system, and SM/PL for use with the National IMP-16 system.

An *editor* is a program that allows the user to make textual changes in his program without reloading or rewriting it. The editor program performs such functions as adding or deleting a line or a character automatically. Editors are quite important, since it must be realized that even a typing error as a program is written out would have to be corrected by retyping the entire program if it was not for the editor.

A *debugger* is a system diagnostic tool that permits the user to analyze the program while it is running. The programmer may insert breakpoints into the program at critical points and obtain information such as register and memory dumps, at specific points of program execution. If the program detects an error, some debugging programs permit the user to make the appropriate modification and to let the program continue to run.

A *loader* is a program that initializes the processor to enable the user program to begin execution. A loader is often provided together with a hardware facility known as a "reset" button. If the processor is halted for some unknown reason, the user can restart operation of a program by pressing the "reset" button. The reset hardware facility then "jams" an appropriate instruction into the processor so that control is taken away from the program formerly executed, and processing of a new program begins. Other types of loaders permits separate groups of machine language code to be linked together and executed by the processor; these more sophisticated types of loaders are referred to as linkage editors.

A *simulator* is a specialized program for performing more sophisticated analyses of user programs. A simulator is designed to model or simulate the timing and characteristics of hardware, such as peripherals, which may not be available for testing at the time the software is tested.

The *PROM programmer* is an independent piece of hardware that is available with many development systems for the purpose of programming ROMs. A PROM programmer simplifies software development since test programs may be represented on PROMs and run on the system without the necessity of loading the program into RAM for each test. A PROM programmer includes such functions as program listing, program by manual keyboard, PROM duplication, and program verification functions.

CHAPTER EIGHT
MICROPROCESSOR
APPLICATIONS

Applications for microprocessors spans the entire range of industrial, commercial, consumer, and institutional applications. In the present chapter, we consider applications in these three areas:

consumer/institutional (low-cost computer)
commercial (point-of-sale terminal)
industrial (automotive controllers)

A LOW-COST GENERAL-PURPOSE COMPUTER

The first major application of the microprocessor in the consumer or institutional market is that of a low-cost general-purpose computer. For under $1000, the consumer or educator may purchase a "microcomputer" that is able to run simple programs, as demonstrations, or perform various tasks. Such a "home computer" is particularly appealing for educational programs, to the electronics hobbyist, or for entertainment such as computerized games.

There are a number of ways in which the home "microcomputer" is sold: to be assembled by the hobbyist, already assembled, and even preprogrammed. The lowest cost microcomputers are those preprogrammed and packaged for a dedicated operation, such as an educational toy. A simple dedicated system could easily sell for less than $200 based on a minimum number of parts and relatively simple system development costs.

An example of a minimum system using the Intel 4040 is shown in Fig. 1. The configuration shown in this figure is about the simplest that can be constructed, consisting merely of the CPU, the clock, a ROM, and an I/O chip.

Such a simple microcomputer is a dedicated processor. The programs to be executed have already been designed and debugged and are stored in the ROM. The user enters his data through the I/O ports through a data entry device such as pushbuttons, toggle switches, a keyboard, or the

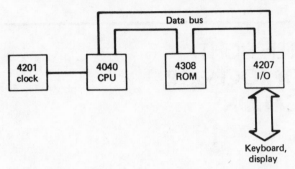

FIGURE 8.1   MINIMAL MICROPROCESSOR SYSTEM.

like, the processor executes it, and supplys the appropriate response to the output port.

More sophisticated systems require more hardware, such as a keyboard and display. Such peripherals have been designed as low-cost components so that they are price-compatible with the microprocessor system. For a display, it is possible to use an ordinary television set provided with the appropriate interface circuits. Such a low-cost development system is shown in Fig. 8.2.

Character Display Device

A simple character display for a television monitor is shown in Fig. 8.3. Most typically the bit patterns for the characters to be displayed are stored in a read-only memory. A television set in the United States operates with 525 lines, scanned at a rate of 30 frames per second. This corresponds to 64 microseconds for each picture line. If we consider, for example, displaying 64 characters in each line, we must provide means for producing

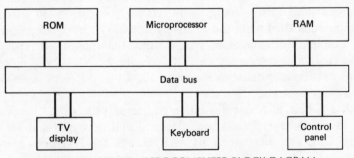

FIGURE 8.2   HOME MICROCOMPUTER BLOCK DAGRAM.

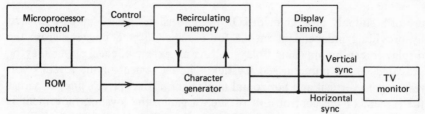

FIGURE 8.3   TV CHARACTER DISPLAY BLOCK DIAGRAM.

one character every microsecond. Shift registers or recirculating memories are provided so that a character which is written on the screen is continually rewritten or refreshed.

The radio frequency portion of the display device consists of circuitry for generating the appropriate RF signal to be supplied to the television monitor. The bit pattern is used to generate a modulating signal that modulates the RF output of a RF signal generator.

Fig. 8.4 shows the display pattern of a series of dots or scanning segments across a picture line.

The arrangement shown in Fig. 8.3 is not limited to merely generating characters. Graphics or other images may be generated and displayed by

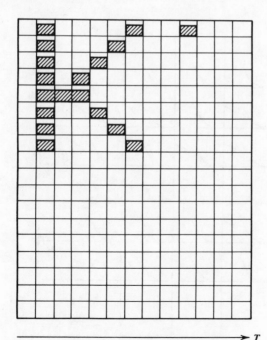

FIGURE 8.4   CHARACTER FORMAT.

use of a suitably programmed ROM. A television "game" may be created by providing independent means for moving discrete images across the display screen by opposing "players." As an example, each player may be provided with a miniaturized joystick. The movement of the joystick corresponds to vertical and horizontal movement of the player's marker across the screen. In the control unit of such a game, the joystick movement is translated into delayed pulses from horizontal and vertical sync signal generators. The delayed pulses are applied to a coincidence gate, and modulate an RF signal which is applied to the television monitor.

Keyboard. Another important input device for the system is a keyboard. A simple numeric keyboard may be used, together with program keys, for arithmetical or calculator type applications, or an alphabet keyboard for more sophisticated word processing applications, including assembly language processing.

An example of the interface to be provided for a keyboard in a microprocessor system is shown in Fig. 8.5. The scanning keyboard encoder

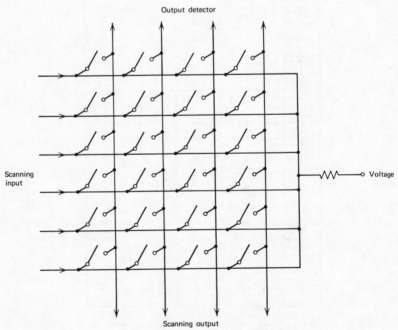

FIGURE 8.5   KEYBOARD ENCODER.

detects key closures and relays the appropriate encoded signal to the micro-processor.

Other peripheral devices may be provided in the system in addition to the TV display and the keyboard, such as an off-line storage facility. The simplest storage facility is the magnetic tape cassette, and it is anticipated that low cost peripherals for a home microcomputer will be developed utilizing ordinary audio cassettes for an off-line storage.

Applications

Applications. It would be worthwhile to list a few of the anticipated applications for the home microcomputer:

educational games and toys
programmable timing and control (appliances, building heating, cooling)
word processing systems
information and record storage

Such applications may be programmed on a general-purpose home micro-computer, or dedicated microcomputers may be supplied as parts of consumer products or appliances. A microcomputer may perform certain routine household functions such as menu planning and cooking programs. A domestic range for household cooking may feature digital controls, displays, timers, and a microprocessor control. A stored program may provide information on the cooking time necessary for various types of meat and may automatically turn on and off various burners or ovens in response to program control. The touch-control panel and display of such a digitally controlled range developed by General Motors is shown in Fig. 8.6.

POINT-OF-SALE TERMINAL

The point-of-sale system is one of the most important commercial appli-cations of microcomputers. The POS terminal is an interactive device that processes sales information and stores it on a magnetic tape cassette.

There are at least two possible inputs of data to the POS terminal:

keyboard
optical symbol reader (scanner)

As shown in Fig. 8.7, these inputs are connected to the system data bus.

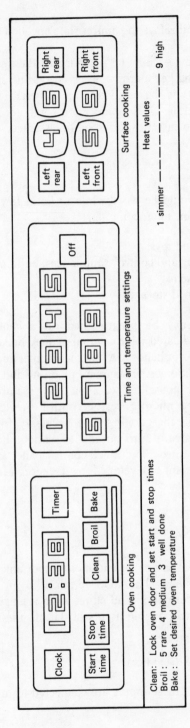

FIGURE 8.6 COOKING RANGE DIGITAL PANEL.

154

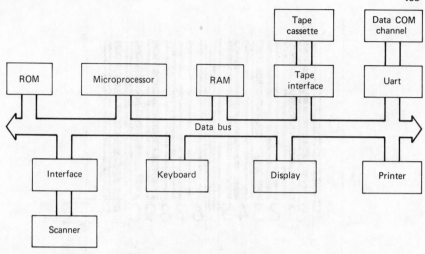

FIGURE 8.7   POINT-OF-SALE TERMINAL.

Also attached to the data bus are the microprocessor, ROM and RAM, and system outputs:

   display
   printer
   tape cassette
   UART for remote transmission of data

The operator specifies the mode of operation (keyboard or scanner) by means of a program key on the keyboard. For normal keyboard operation, the POS terminal acts as a normal cash register, recording the sales and providing a display for visual verification and a printed receipt. For operation with the optical scanner, more sophisticated processing operations are required.

In connection with scanners for POS terminals, it would be worthwhile to indicate the symbol specification of one widely used symbol—the Universal Product Code (UPC) symbol of the supermarket industry. The basic definition of the UPC symbol is illustrated in Fig. 8.8.

The UPC symbol is a means for providing automated reading of product information in a point of sale system. The UPC symbol, as shown in Fig. 8.8 contains 10 digits of information divided into two 5-digit fields. The data in these fields are also represented as numerals in OCR-B font below the symbol. In the specific representation of Fig. 8.8, the left-hand 5-digit field contains the characters 12345, and the right-hand 5-digit field contains the characters 67890.

FIGURE 8.8 UPC SYMBOL (COPYRIGHT 1975 UNIFORM PRODUCT CODE COUNCIL, INC.).

In its application in the grocery industry, the left-hand five digits serves to identify the manufacturer of the product, while the right-hand five digits serves to identify the product itself.

The representation of a specific digit in the UPC symbol is best explained with reference to Fig. 8.9. Each character position consists of a region of seven "modules" or bar positions. A dark bar represents a 1-bit, while a light bar represents a 0-bit. Thus the code represented by the character

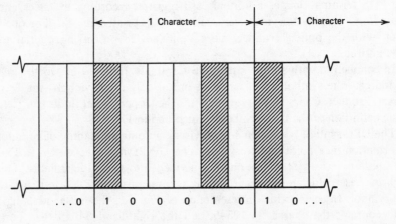

FIGURE 8.9 UPC CHARACTER REPRESENTATION.

shown in Fig. 8.9 has bits 1000100. To decode this bit string, one looks
on the table in Fig. 8.10, which indicates the decimal value 7.

As shown in Fig. 8.10, there is a distinction between "left characters"
(i.e., the characters in the left-hand five-digit field), and "right characters"
(i.e., the characters in the right-hand five-digit field). This distinction is
made to permit the symbol to be read in either direction. By encoding a
specific parity in the characters of the right and the left digits fields, the
POS terminal may automatically determine which way the symbol is being
read and interpret the data accordingly.

Other characteristics of the UPC symbol should also be noted. Each
character consists of two dark bands, and two light bands, where each
band is composed of one, two, three, or four bars or modules of the
same color.

A description of the guard and check patterns of the UPC symbol are
presented in Fig. 8.11. On the far left-hand side of the symbol is a numeral
that designates the code being used. A "0" refers to the UPC code presented above; "3" refers to the National Drug Code; and so on. In the
left-hand portion of the symbol is a guard bar pattern 101, followed by
the number system character, in this case "0" or 0001101. The left five
characters of the code are presented, followed by the center bar pattern
01010. Immediately to the right of the center bar pattern is the right five
characters, followed by a modulo check character, in this case 1001110,
followed by the right-hand guard pattern 101.

The scanning hardware and microprocessor system may be designed to

Decimal value	Left characters	Right characters
	(Odd parity—0)	(Even parity—E)
0	0001101	1110010
1	0011001	1100110
2	0010011	1101100
3	0111101	1000010
4	0100011	0011100
5	0110001	0001110
6	0101111	1010000
7	0111011	1000100
8	0110111	1001000
9	0001011	1110100

FIGURE 8.10 UPC CHARACTER CODE.

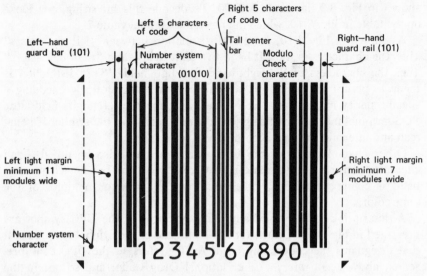

FIGURE 8.11   UPC SYMBOL SPECIFICATION.

handle the UPC symbol format, and be provided with appropriate read-only memories containing a character look-up table. Should the code be changed, for example, to be able to handle the National Drug Code, the user need only replace the read-only memory with the new memory containing a different look-up table. The economic advantages and versatility of a microprocessor implementation of a POS system should not be overlooked by all segments of the consumer transactions industry.

AUTOMOTIVE APPLICATIONS

The use of microprocessors as on-board vehicle controllers is one of the most publicized and potentially important applications of microprocessors.

Automotive electronics is an extremely active area of research by automotive companies. The operating environment of an automobile engine presents considerable challenge for the electronics system designer. This is not to say, however, that both active and passive components are not already widely used in automotive systems. Figure 8.12 presents an estimate of the number of electronic components used on existing electronic systems used in automobiles.

The applications for microprocessors in the automobile are numerous. Figure 8.13 presents a rather detailed listing of various potential appli-

Estimate of electronic components
on existing systems

System	Active	Resistors	Capacitors
Alternator	6	—	—
Voltage regulator	5	5	1
Electronic fuel injection		160	10
Electronic ignition	15	15	2
Intermittent windshield wiper	5	5	2
Cruise control	60	105	15
Wheel lock control	185	290	40
Traction control	40	80	10
Headlamp dimmer	15	25	5
Climate control	5	15	1
Air cushion restraint	95	100	15
Digital clock	200	220	35
Totals	706	1,020	136

Source: General Motors.

FIGURE 8.12   AUTOMATIC ELECTRONIC COMPONENTS.

cations as compiled by General Motors Corporation. The figure also indicates the major developments required before such systems are feasible, as well as the current barriers to be overcome.

Some of the areas of initial developmental research are:

ignition timing
exhaust gas recirculation
fuel usage measurements

A simple block diagram that illustrates the various operations of an automotive microprocessor system is shown in Fig. 8.13. The four inputs to the microprocessor system are:

pressure
temperature
RPM
EGR valve position

These inputs are provided by means of transducers or sensors located within the engine or EGR valve itself. As the data presented in Fig. 8.13 indicate, some of the most difficult problems to be overcome in the develop-

Proposed Automotive Electronic Systems

SYSTEM		MAJOR DEVELOPMENT REQUIRED				MAJOR BARRIER		
		TRANSDUCER	PROCESSOR	ACTUATOR	DISPLAY	COST	TECHNICAL	OTHER
AUTOMATIC DOOR LOCKS				X		X		
ALCOHOL DETECTION SYSTEMS		X			X	X	X	X
FLASHER CONTROL SYSTEMS				X		X		
PROGRAMMED DRIVING CONTROLS			X	X		X	X	
HIGH SPEED WARNING						X		
HIGH SPEED LIMITING				X		X		
LAMP MONITOR SYSTEMS		X				X		
ELECTRONIC HORN						X		
CRASH RECORDER		X	X		X	X	X	X
TRAFFIC CONTROLS		X	X	X	X	X	X	X
TIRE PRESSURE MONITOR		X				X		
TIRE PRESSURE CONTROL		X		X		X	X	
AUTOMATIC SEAT POSITIONER						X		
AUTOMATIC MIRROR CONTROL		X		X		X	X	
AUTOMATIC ICING CONTROL		X				X	X	
ROAD SURFACE INDICATOR		X			X	X		
4 WHEEL ANTI-LOCK				X		X		
VEHICLE GUIDANCE		X		X		X	X	X
STATION KEEPING	RADAR	X		X		X	X	
	INFRA-RED	X		X		X	X	
	LASER	X		X		X	X	
	SONIC	X		X		X	X	
AUTOMATIC BRAKES	RADAR	X	X	X			X	
	INFRA-RED	X	X	X			X	
	LASER	X	X	X			X	
	SONIC	X	X	X			X	
PREDICTIVE CRASH SENSORS	RADAR	X				X	X	
	INFRA-RED	X				X	X	
	LASER	X				X	X	
	SONIC	X				X	X	
ELECTRONIC TIMING						X		
MULTIPLEX HARNESS SYSTEMS				X		X		
ELECTRONIC TRANSMISSION CONTROL				X		X		
ELECTRONIC COOLING SYS. CONTROL				X		X		
CLOSED LOOP EMISSION CONTROL		X		X		X	X	
ACCESSORY POWER CONTROL		X		X		X		
CRUISE CONTROL				X				
THEFT DETERRENT SYSTEMS		X				X		
ON BOARD DIAGNOSTIC SYSTEMS		X				X		X
OFF BOARD DIAGNOSTIC SYSTEMS		X				X		X
LEVELING CONTROLS		X		X		X		
RADIO FREQUENCY DISPLAY						X		
DIGITAL SPEEDOMETERS					X	X		
DIGITAL TACHOMETERS					X	X		
ELAPSED TIME CLOCK					X	X		
ELECTRONIC ODOMETER					X	X		
TRIP ODOMETER					X	X		
DESTINATION MILEAGE					X	X		
MILES PER GALLON		X			X	X		
MILES TO GO		X			X	X		
ESTIMATED ARRIVAL TIME					X	X		
TRIP FUEL CONSUMPTION		X			X	X		
AVERAGE SPEED					X	X		
AVERAGE MILES PER GALLON					X	X		
DIGITAL FUEL GAGE					X	X		
SERVICE INTERVAL					X	X		
DIGITAL TEMPERATURE GAGES					X	X		
DIGITAL PRESSURE GAGES					X	X		
DIGITAL VOLTMETER					X	X		
DIGITAL METRIC CONVERSIONS					X	X		
ACCELERATION GAGE		X			X	X		
DRUNK DRIVERS		X	X				X	X
E.K.G.		X	X	X		X	X	X
SLEEP DETECTORS		X	X				X	X

Source: General Motors

FIGURE 8.13 AUTOMOTIVE APPLICATIONS OF MICROPROCESSORS.

ment of microprocessor systems for automotive applications are in the design of such transducers.

Assuming that reliable transducers will be developed, they will provide analog input signals that are multiplexed and converted to digital signals for use by the processor. Such digital signals may be temporarily stored

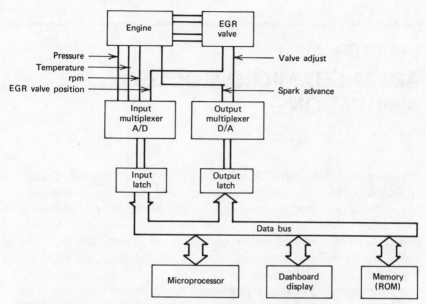

FIGURE 8.14 AUTOMOTIVE MICROCOMPUTER SYSTEM BLOCK DIAGRAM.

in input latches until they are to be displayed or processed. The input latches are connected to the microprocessor along the system data bus.

The outputs are either to an actuator for performing an engine control operation, or to a dashboard display for routine monitoring of engine conditions or alerting of predetermined critical conditions. The actuators shown in Fig. 8.14 indicates the spark advance and EGR value position adjustment. The particular nature of these adjustments, depending on the type of automobile and its operating environment, may be predetermined by the manufacturer and specified with specific parameters that are permanently stored in the ROM. The microprocessor responds with suitable engine adjustments on the basis of the stored information together with concurrent operating conditions sensed from the engine.

CHAPTER NINE
ADVANCED MICROPROCESSOR
APPLICATIONS

Microprocessors may also be utilized in fairly sophisticated electronics applications, including telecommunications and multiprocessor systems.

Telecommunications is expected to be one of the most important areas for the future application of microprocessors. Information processing is important in all stages of a telecommunications system, and the low-cost dedicated capabilities of microprocessors can be fully exploited in an integrated communications system.

Multiprocessor systems, or large-scale data-processing systems utilizing microprocessors for performing certain processing functions, are somewhat less important. The low-cost processing capabilities make the use of microprocessors particularly attractive in larger scale computer systems, but other factors may mitigate against their use. Since the number of such large-scale multiprocessor systems is relatively small, there may not be enough commercial justification to design machine architectures based on low-cost microprocessors. However, from at least an academic standpoint, the discussion of microprocessors in large-scale data systems is worthwhile.

TELECOMMUNICATIONS

Telecommunications is expected to be one of the most fruitful areas for microprocessor applications. There are a number of important fields to consider:

> large-scale computer networks
> telephony applications
> identification systems

Large-Scale Computer Networks

The development of large-scale computer networks coincidentally with microprocessor technology is not really paradoxical. Large-scale computers and associated networks are directed at a narrow market of specialized users concerned with large data bases or distributed interactive users. This market includes many banking and financial applications, insurance, retailers, distribution firms, and reservation systems. Although the market for such applications is a narrow one, it is large and growing, both in terms of the number of users and the services it is expected to provide. Data processing requirements of smaller businesses typically do not require the transfer of data from one location to another. The implementation of data processing capabilities for such users, including through the use of microprocessors, is an area of totally different machine specifications and market characteristics.

Data communication systems may be used to implement a wide variety of specialized data processing applications:

message switching
file management
inquiry/response systems
data collection
remote batch

Message switching refers to the processing and communication of messages over limited channel capacity systems.

File management refers to the remote updating of a centralized file, or other file handling and processing functions from a remote location.

Inquiry/response systems are another form of file oriented system, in which a remote station makes inquiries of a centralized file but does not have the capabilities to change that file.

Data collection refers to the use of a remore station to provide updated or current information to a centralized file.

Remote batch is the use of a data communications facility to batch enter a series of jobs into a remote central processing unit.

In designing a data communications system, the system designer must carefully integrate each of the component technologies:

transmission technology
communications technology
network structure and technology

The transmission technology merely refers to the means for transmitting the signals. In telephone communications, for example, one would refer to the grade of the line (low-speed, voice, broadband), or type (private, switched, WATS, etc.). Of course there are now a number of important alternatives to telephone communications, including microwave and satellite transmission links.

Data communication presently accounts for about 15% of the usage of the public telephone network, a relatively small percentage that is expected to grow to about 30% by 1980. Projections of usage for specialized communications services, such as data communication or videotelephone, have always been overly optimistic, both inside and outside of the Bell System or other carriers. The growth in data communication has been affected by a number of factors:

relatively high communications costs
variety of processing systems and procedures
sharply lower prices of stand-alone data processing capabilities
alternative transmission technologies
regulatory and competitive factors

There are two basic types of data communications:

direct data transmission
concentrated data transmission

Direct data transmission refers to the use of a single line or communications channel for the transmission of data. Such an arrangement is the simplest kind and is most suitable for handling a predetermined volume of message traffic. If more than one user desires to utilize the communications channel, some form of multiplexing is used, such as frequency-division multiplexing (FDM) or time-division multiplexing (TDM).

Concentrated data transmission refers to the use of store-and-forward techniques for handling messages. These techniques include message switching and packet switching.

Message switching refers to the accumulation of a message in a store until a complete message has been assembled, and then transmitting it to the next destination when a data link becomes available. Message switching is thus distinguished from circuit switching in which no intermediate storage takes place. In circuit switching, if a line or data link is not available, the service request must be repeated again.

Packet switching refers to the formation of messages into a "packet" having a predetermined length.

The basic role of a microprocessor in a data communication system is that of acting as a communication processor. The role of a communication processor is to interface or "front end" the host processor (the large-scale computer and terminal) with the communication channel, as shown in Fig. 9.1. Some of the functions of a communication processor are:

scheduling
data compression

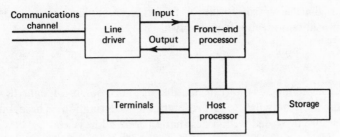

FIGURE 9.1   COMMUNICATIONS PROCESSOR.

polling
storage and buffering
data link control
code conversion
formatting

Many of these functions are now performed by minicomputers. However, a minicomputer has far greater speed and processing capabilities
than is necessary to handle these routine processing tasks. Dedicated
microprocessors would be much more efficient and cost effective in such
applications.

Microprocessors may be utilized to perform a number of distinct functions in a data communication system.

protocol handling
error code generating and checking
packet and message formation
receiver/transmitter control
synchronization
automatic repeat request (ARQ) or forward error correction (FEC)
multiple access control, that is,
    time-division multiple access (TDMA)
    frequency-division multiple access (FDMA)
    space-division multiple access (SDMA)
    code-division multiple access (CDMA)

The best way to illustrate how a microprocessor is utilized in a data
communications system is to take a specific example: that of a data link
interface processor in a packet communication system.

Packet Communication.   Packet communication, based on the transmission of message "packets," was originally proposed in the early 1960s.

There are basically two forms of packet communications, distinguished by the transmission technology involved:

packet switching
packet broadcasting

Packet switching is the transmission of short bursts of data through a communication network to a predetermined destination. These bursts of "packets" are provided with a destination code address and are "switched" through network nodes until the destination is reached. Such packet switches take place over a linked-node communication network.

Packet broadcasting is the simultaneous transmission of a packet to several remote stations. Each remote station is equipped with decoding equipment that decodes every incoming packet to determine whether it is addressed to that station. Packet broadcasting can therefore be realized as a radio broadcasting communication system.

A packet broadcasting system may be implemented by means of a satellite transmission network. The increased availability and decreasing cost of satellite communication is an important aspect of the growth of long-range data communication. Some of the key advantages of satellite transmission are:

communication costs being independent of the distance
data transmission via broadcasting rather than switching through a
    network
high speed (30 megabits per second) capabilities

There are a few drawbacks to satellite communication systems, such as the time delay as the signal is transmitted up-link and down-link, and possible signal attenuation during precipitation or other conditions.

Packet broadcasting may also be realized on wire channels, in loops or other interconnection schemes.

The ALOHA System of the University of Hawaii is one such packet broadcasting system using packet broadcasting ground-based and satellite-based channels. Information is transmitted to the satellite from an earth station in short digital bursts. The repeater on the satellite picks up these transmissions and "broadcasts" them over a predetermined region of the earth's surface. Ground stations throughout the region intercept these broadcasts, decode the address or header information on the packets, and select those packets labeled for that destination for further processing.

An application of the microprocessor to a packet communications system in development in the United Kingdom is described in the next section.

Microcomputer Application: Data Link Interface Processor in Packet Communication System.   An actual example of the use of a microprocessor system in a packet switched data communication network can now be described. The particular application in the system is a data link interface communication processor. The basic block diagram of the system is shown in Fig. 9.2. The communication processor links the transmission lines with a buffer store which is connected with the Host or central processor. The user of the system interfaces with the central processor through a terminal or tape reader.

The block diagram of the interface unit is shown in Fig. 9.3. The microprocessor (in this case a National IMP-16) is connected by means of

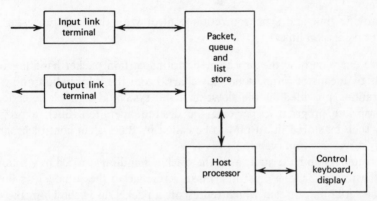

FIGURE 9.2   PACKET COMMUNICATIONS SYSTEM DATA LINK INTERFACE.

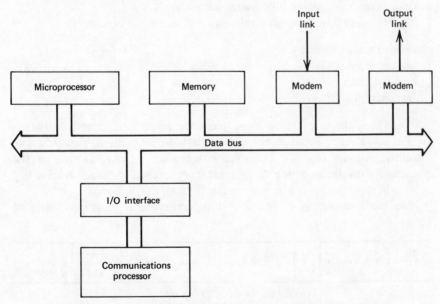

FIGURE 9.3   DATA LINK INTERFACE PROCESSOR BLOCK DIAGRAM.

control, address, and data busses to memory and interface units. The data link interface performs the following functions:

perform serial/parallel conversion between the transmission link and the processor

perform routine error checking, such as the arithmetic check sum and cyclic redundancy check

provide header and frame information on outgoing data and strip the header and frame information from incoming data

assemble the data into packets of predetermined size by means of a data buffer

provide link and synchronization control with the host processor and the transmission link.

We examine how the processor performs certain packet handling functions by means of a functional flowchart. From the information on system operations provided in the flowchart, the system designer can code the appropriate program to perform the desired operation. Such a program may then be stored in a ROM to be called by the system control program, or by direct user intervention.

To understand the nature of the packet handling procedures followed by the processor, one must first make reference to the protocol or format of the serial data stream which represents a packet, as is shown in Fig. 9.4.

The various control characters represented in Fig. 9.4 as SYN, DLE, and so on refer to specific bit pattern sequences.

The program flow depends on the value of a number of flags:

synchronous idle flag
packet receive flag
end-of-packet
transparent DLE

The specification of when these flags are set is determined by means of a routine represented in the state transition diagram of Fig. 9.5. The synchronous idle flag, for example, is set when synchronization of the processor with the incoming data stream is achieved. The packet receive flag is set when the packet framing character is received.

The basic operation of the data link control unit may be illustrated

...	S S Y Y N N	...	S Y N	D L E	S T X	Header	Message	D L E	E T X	Error check bits	S S S Y Y Y N N N	...

FIGURE 9.4 PACKET FORMAT.

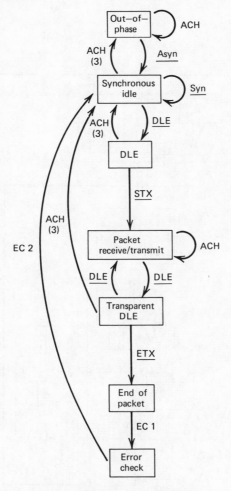

Note (1) ACH = Any character not specified.
(2) Underlined characters are specified control characters.
(3) Error condition.

FIGURE 9.5 STATE TRANSITION DIAGRAM (REPRINTED, BY PERMISSION, FROM HALSALL, *THE RADIO AND ELECTRONIC ENGINEER*).

with reference to the flowchart of Fig. 9.6. The flowchart makes reference to the input shift register which converts the serial data stream to parallel format. The data in the shift register are transferred from the shift register to the A-register of the processor by means of an exchange. The particular route through the flowchart is determined from which of the flags are set.

As shown in the flowchart, if the synchronous idle flag is not set, a

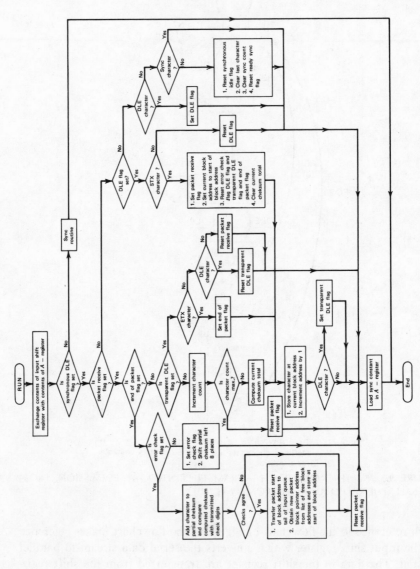

FIGURE 9.6 FLOW CHART (REPRINTED, BY PERMISSION, FROM HALSALL, *The Radio and Electronic Engineer*).

170

synchronization ("SYNC") routine is entered to synchronize operation. The packet-receive flag is checked next. As shown in Fig. 9.6, the packet-rceive flag is set when a DLE followed by a STX character is received and remains set while the packet message is received.

One follows the flowchart in a vertical direction to indicate how each character in the packet message is processed. The fact that the "packet-receive" flag is set while the "end of packet" flag is not set indicates that the characters being received are part of the packet message.

The transparent DLE flag is checked next. The DLE character is a specific bit sequence that may occur in the middle of a packet message as data. To avoid confusion between data and a DLE protocol character, there is a rule that any DLE bit-sequence in the packet message itself is repeated. Such repeated DLE bit-sequences are detected and translated into the correct data that they represent for storage. This is done by bypassing the storage step when the second DLE bit-sequence is received, as shown in the flowchart branch to the right of the "Is transparent DLE flag set?" decision box.

Assuming the transparent DLE flag is not set, the character count is incremented. If the maximum character count has not yet been reached, the current checksum is calculated. The checksums are updated for each character received until, at the end of the packet, the total checksum is compared with the transmitted check digits. This routine is expressed in the flowchart branch to the left of the "Is end of packet flag set?" decision box.

The transmitted packet message character is then stored at the current block address, and the system continues to process subsequent characters.

One of the most critical aspects of communication processor systems design is speed. Table 9.1 indicates the processor time and storage requirements for the error checking operations of the National IMP-16 system:

TABLE 9.1 NATIONAL IMP-16 SYSTEM PROCESSOR TIME AND STORAGE REQUIREMENTS FOR ERROR CHECKING OPERATIONS.

	Maximum processing time per character (microseconds)	Program storage requirement (words)
Input operation		
Arithmetic Checksum	455.7	227
Cyclic Redundancy Check	1096.2	262
Output operation		
Arithmetic Checksum	273.8	135
Cyclic Redundancy Check	1371.6	172

The amount of time and storage requirements for the cyclic redundancy check calculation are higher because of the greater number of operations required per character. The processing time requirements place a constraint on the transmission speeds which can be handled using a microcomputer system.

Telephony Applications

The use of microprocessors in telephony applications is anticipated to be a very promising area. There are a number of distinct applications where the capabilities and low cost of microprocessors offer significant advantages over other technologies. The particular applications that we should consider in greater detail are:

> switching systems
> digital speech encoding
> digital filters
> transaction telephone systems

In addition to the applications above, another important area is the field of computer communications through the switched telephone network. The particular application of microprocessors to such data communications is more fully reviewed in the section on large-scale computer networks above.

Telephone Switching Systems. A telephone switching system provides communication links between specified lines in response to subscriber requests. Switching systems range in size from small PABX (private automated branch exchange) systems with under 100 lines, to central office or tandem systems handling tens of thousands of lines.

A detailed block diagram of a central office telephone switching system is shown in Fig. 9.7. The block diagram shows the two main elements of the system—the switching network and the central processor.

The switching network is the means for selectively interconnecting two-wire metallic paths by means of internal junctor circuits. Such interconnections effect a communication path between a subscriber station (the telephone shown in the lefthand portion of Fig. 9.7) and a trunk that connects to other central offices.

There are a number of potential applications of microprocessors to a telephone switching system. Most notable are those peripheral or administrative functions that are functionally independent of overall system control.

Microprocessors may be utilized to implement special call facilities as part of the signal processor system or to control administrative routines. These administrative routines periodically preform diagnostic routines

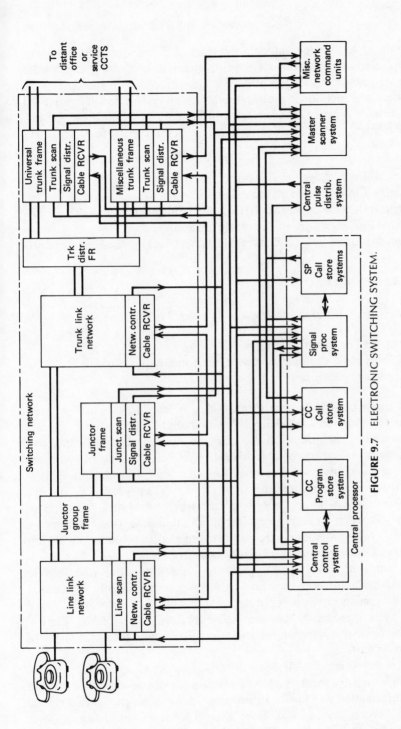

FIGURE 9.7 ELECTRONIC SWITCHING SYSTEM.

173

through the system to determine the presence of primary or secondary malfunctions. Such routines do not require extensive processing capabilities and are well within the capabilities of a microprocessor to handle.

The Central Processor is a centralized data processing facility employed to implement the varied telephone, maintenance, and administrative functions of a telephone switching system. The Central Processor is divided into five basic elements:

1. Central Control System (main processor)
2. Central Control Program Store System
3. Central Control Call Store System (main processor memory)
4. Signal Processor System (auxiliary processor)
5. Signal Processor Call Store System (auxiliary processor memory).

Central Control System

Functionally, Central Control System is divided into three parts:

1. Basic data processing facilities
2. Facilities for communicating with input and output equipment
3. Maintenance facilities.

The Central Control System includes two independent central controls for purposes of system reliability. The independent central controls are both arranged to perform all of the necessary system actions. In the most usual mode of operation, both independent central controls carry on the same work functions on the basis of duplicate input information. This is termed the in-step mode of operation. However, only one of the two central controls can alter the system status or control the execution of telephone functions at any given instant. That is, the two independent central controls provide control and maintenance information to the remainder of the system on a mutually exclusive basis.

The Central Control System performs data processing functions in accordance with program orders that are stored principally in Central Control Program Store System. In response to a program order, the Central Control System processes data generally obtained from Central Control Call Store System and generates and transmits signals for the control of other system units.

The Central Control Call Store System is a word-organized random-access high-capacity memory system wherein certain of the more volatile system information is stored. Information can be written into or read from the Central Control Call Store System by the Central Control System. Since information in the Central Control Call Store System is readily changed at the normal system speed, the more volatile system information is stored therein. This information includes:

1. Information relating to calls, as received from signal processor system (e.g., call signaling information).
2. Information relating to recent changes in directory number to line equipment number translations.
3. Recent changes in subscriber class of service information.
4. System administrative information.
5. Subscriber and trunk busy-idle information.
6. Network path busy-idle information.
7. System work lists and queues.

A microprocessor may be implemented at various points in the Central Control System to perform specific processing functions that were previously performed by a central processor on a periodic basis. By dedicating a single inexpensive processor to a single function, a considerable amount of efficiency is gained.

Signal Processor System

Signal Processor System is a special purpose data processing facility employed to implement those repetitive and time consuming input and output system functions which, if performed exclusively by Central Control System, would limit the call handling capacity of the telephone system. The Signal Processor System, although functionally independent, is subject to the command of the Central Control System and communicates to the Central Control System that information necessary to perform the more complex data processing required for call processing and system maintenance.

The Signal Processor Call Store System is a word-organized random-access high-capacity memory system wherein the program for controlling the Signal Processor System and the data upon which the Signal Processor System operates are stored. Each signal processor community of the signal processor system is discretely associated with a separate signal processor call store system. Accordingly, if more than one signal processor community is included in the signal processor system, a corresponding number of signal processor call systems is provided.

The information stored in the signal processor call store system includes:

1. The program of instruction words that controls the operation of the signal processor system when the signal processor system is not responding to commands from the central control system.
2. The data generated and utilized by the signal processor system in carrying out its programmed data processing operations.

Accordingly, the information stored in the signal processor call store system is a mixture of instruction words and data words. Among the types of data stored in the signal processor call store system are:

1. Information relating to calls, such as supervisory change of state information, which is received from the switching network and miscellaneous administrative circuits of the switching system.
2. Information relating to calls which is received by way of the signal processor system from the central control system for processing by the signal processor system.
3. System work lists and queues.

Microprocessors may also be used to implement many of the functions of the Signal Processor System, most particularly the testing, supervisory, and adminstrative routines.

Communications Within the Switching System

A plurality of bus systems and cable systems provide the communication paths for transmitting control signals and information between the elements of the central processor and between the central processor and various other divisions of the switching system. In general, a bus system includes two duplicate buses designated bus 0 and bus 1, each comprising a plurality of pairs of conductors that are transformer-coupled between an information source or sources and an information destination or destinations. Data are transmitted over a bus in parallel in the form of short pulses that arrive at the information destination at a common time.

Multiconductor cables provide discrete bidirectional communications paths between selected divisions of the central processor and other divisions of the switching system. The conductor pairs of these cables are either transformer coupled or directly connected to the source of control signals and the destination thereof.

Digital Speech Encoding.   Digital speech encoding is an important aspect of the development of digital facilities in the switched telephone network. Digital intertoll transmission of ordinary voice telephone communications is anticipated to be an extremely impotant area of microprocessor applications. The use of digital facilities for voice transmission is essentially a matter of economics and volume of long-distance calls.

There are essentially two types of digital speech encoding:

delta modulation
pulse code modulation (PCM)

Delta modulation is based on comparing the input analog signal with a reference signal on a periodic basis. Depending on the result of the comparison, a digital 1 or 0 is transmitted. The reference signal is most typically obtained by means of a feedback loop from previous input signals.

The simple delta modulator has a limited dynamic range and thus a number of adaptive techniques have been devised to overcome this limitation. Most of the adaptive techniques increase the dynamic range by increasing the step size or magnitude of the reference level each time the comparison results in an answer similar to the one just previously obtained. That is, if on the first comparison the reference signal is less than the input signal, the reference level is increased by a certain step size. On the next comparison if the reference level is still less than the input signal, the step size itself is increased, thus increasing the reference level for an even greater amount than on the first comparison. This type of delta modulator is called a variable solpe delta modulator (VSD modulator).

The continuously variable slope delta modulator (CVSD modulator) is a variation of the VSD modulator in which the comparison signal, which is indicative of the slope of the analog input signal, is smoothed through a low-pass filter with a bandwidth corresponding to the maximum syllabic rate of human speech, approximately 25 to 35 hertz.

PCM is based on sampling the input analog waveform at a predetermined rate, quantizing each sample, and coding it in terms of a sequence of pulses.

Microprocessors may be utilized in a delta modulation or PCM transmission system for numerous control and monitoring functions. By representing the sampling, testing, storing, and conversion functions as a program, a microprocessor is able to eliminate considerable hardware, as well as permitting monitoring or testing operations to be performed.

In the United States, the Bell System utilizes a digital PCM carrier known as T1 operating at 1.544 megabits per second. The T1 carrier is then multiplexed digitally into a T2 carrier operating at 6.312 megabits per second. The T1 carrier system is part of a digital hierarchy of digital transmission systems shown in Fig 9.8. The T1 carrier system carries 24 voice frequency channels by means of time-division multiplex. Each voice frequency channel is sampled 8000 times per second, produced a 7-bit PCM word which is incorporated together with a 1-bit signal bit field. Each voice channel thus accounts for 64 kilobits second. The basic frame of the T1 system is shown in Fig. 9.9.

Transaction Telephone™. The Transaction Telephone is a business telephone set that permits small or medium sized retail establishments to check the validity of a credit card purchase through the ordinary switched telephone network. The telephone therefore differs from other credit vali-

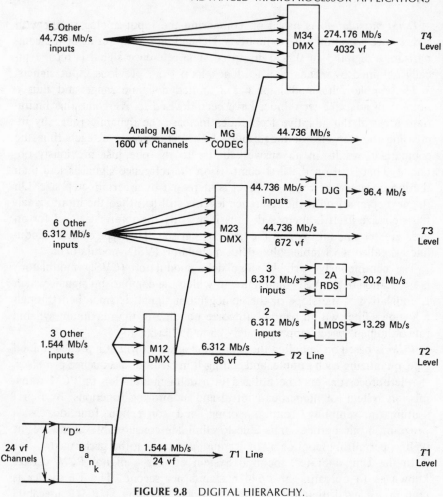

FIGURE 9.8   DIGITAL HIERARCHY.

dation systems that require a dedicated line to the central computer or an acoustical coupler to an ordinary telephone set.

The Transaction Telephone, developed by Bell Telephone Laboratories, utilizes the Rockwell PPS-4 microprocessor together with other Western Electric components.

The Rockwell PPS-4 (i.e., 4-bit Parallel Processing System) was originally introduced in 1972 and marketed primarily to large scale OEM manufacturers, such as the Bell System. The PPS-4 includes a 4-bit CPU based on *p*-channel MOS technology, packaged in a 42-pin flat pack.

The Transaction Telephone operates by the user inserting a credit card

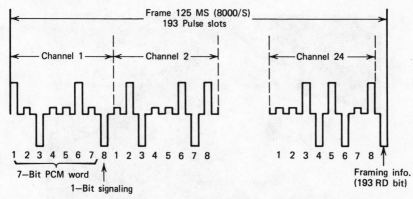

FIGURE 9.9 PCM FRAME OF T1 SYSTEM.

into the card reader on the telephone, as shown in Fig. 9.10. The card reader senses the data contained on the magnetic stripe on the credit card and converts the data into digital signals. The microprocessor determines whether the card has been read correctly by performing a parity check of the read information. If the card has been read correctly, the microprocessor then interprets the data to operate the touch-tone oscillators of the telephone set, sending the data over the telephone network to an on-line computer at the other end. After the remote computer performs a validity check of the serial number of the card, a signal is sent back to the Transaction Telephone indicating whether credit should be authorized or not. The microprocessor receives and interprets this signal and actuates a light on the panel of the telephone to visually indicate to the user whether the transaction is authorized or not.

Although the Transaction Telephone is being marketed to retail establishments for credit validation purposes, consumer use of the product has also been tested. Bank customers, for example, would be able to automatically check their account balances by inserting their bank credit card into a Transaction Telephone equipped with a numeric display. Electronic funds transfer would also be possible through a Transaction Telephone: orders may be placed by phone, and the caller's identity and credit authorization checked remotely.

The Transaction Telephone and similar consumer oriented applications of microprocessors are expected to develop slowly, but their importance cannot be underestimated.

Digital Filters. Digital filters are devices that produce a predetermined digital output in response to a given digital input. They find application in telephony, radar, and signal processing, and are an important area for

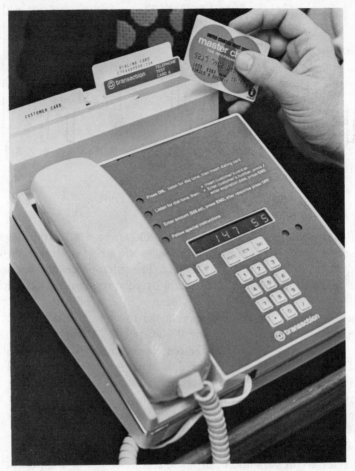

FIGURE 9.10   THE TRANSACTION TELEPHONE™.

the potential application of microprocessors. A digital filter consists of elements for multiplication, addition, delay, and storage, to obtain a predetermined transfer function on a given input digital signal.

There are two basic types of digital filters:

recursive
nonrecursive

A *recursive* filter utilizes a feedback configuration to provide input signals utilizing previously calculated outputs. In a *nonrecursive* filter only the input to the filter is used to determine the output signals.

Fig. 9.11 is a prototype of a microprocessor applied to a recursive digi-

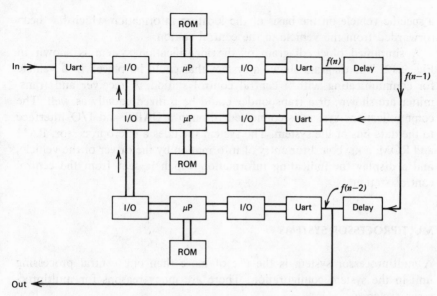

FIGURE 9.11 MICROPROCESSOR CONTROLLED DIGITAL FILTER.

tal filter. The microprocessor and its associated ROM replaces the coefficient generator, multipliers, and adders of the usual hardwired digital filter. The three microprocessors in this particular example are synchronized and connected by means of the I/O interface along a common data bus. The recursive nature of the data applied to the three microprocessors is indicated in the right-hand portion of the figure, where particular points of the circuit represent functional values $f(n)$, $f(n-1)$, and $f(n-2)$.

In addition to the usual filtering functions noted above, the microprocessor may be programmed for performing error checking, formatting, and similar functions. The microprocessor has the capability of changing the transfer function or other filtering characteristics by a simple change in the stored system control program. The flexibility of merely changing a ROM for changing the filtering function or characteristics is the key advantage of the microprocessor implementation.

Identification Systems

Identification systems are another important area of growth for microprocessor applications. Such systems are used to monitor or control the location of moving vehicles, such as trains, buses, police, or other service vehicles, from a central location. The operator may transfer commands to a specific vehicle on the basis of the location information which has been forwarded from the vehicle to the central station.

A simplified block diagram of the identification system is shown in Fig. 9.12. The diagram shows a system that could be placed in a vehicle for communicating with a central control station. A receiver and transmitter are shown, or a transponder could be utilized equally as well. The communications system is connected through a UART and I/O interface to the data bus of the system. The system includes a microprocessor, RAM and ROM, a keyboard for entry of information by the driver of the vehicle, and a display for indicating information which is sent from the central control station.

MULTIPROCESSOR SYSTEMS

A multiprocessor system is the use of more than one central processing unit in the system configuration. There are many reasons for multiprocessor systems:

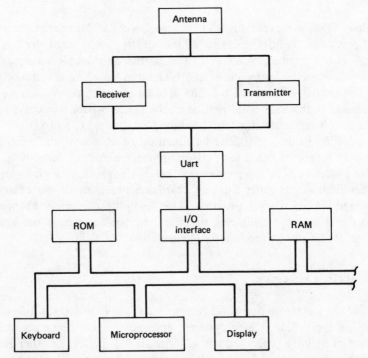

FIGURE 9.12   MICROPROCESSOR CONTROLLED IDENTIFICATION SYSTEM.

greater system efficiency and use of system resources

increase in system capabilities in responding to real time situations

fault tolerance: the greater ability to deal with system malfunctions

There are a number of different ways to classify multiprocessor systems, based on the following characteristics:

the types of processors (i.e., the same or having different characteristics)

the interconnections between processors

the relationship of the processors to memory and I/O units

operating software for the processors and the system

On the basis of these characteristics, one can refer to certain processors as being "array" processors, "pipeline" processors, "parallel" processors, "ring" processors, or "reconfigurable" processors. One can also describe the system structure as being "tightly coupled" or "loosely coupled."

Although microprocessors may be utilized for various functions in a multiprocessor computer system, the most interesting concept is a multiprocessor system constructed of a plurality of microprocessors. The particular type of multiprocessor architecture that is particularly worth considering is a reconfigurable architecture using microprocessors.

Reconfigurable Microprocessor Architectures

The concept of a reconfigurable data processing system is not new. Elements of both hardware and software reconfigurability are well known in multiprocessor systems. It was not, however, until the widespread availability of low cost central processing units in the form of microprocessors that reconfigurable computer architectures became economically feasible.

A multiprocessor computer system in its most basic form consists of a plurality of processors, memory units, and I/O devices arranged in a predetermined configuration. At certain times it may be desirable to change this configuration based on a particular internal or external event. A computer system which posseses the hardware or software capabilities to implement such reconfiguration is called a reconfigurable architecture.

There are a number of important applications for reconfigurable computer systems:

fault-tolerant systems

interactive multiprocessor systems

configurable array processors

compiler-based systems

Fault tolerant systems find their most important application in high reliability systems, such as communications and telephony processing equipment. Such equipment must perform these important fault-handling processing functions:

error detection and localization
restriction of error propagation
recovery

The system must "reconfigure" all data flow around the particular unit which is apparently at fault, be that unit a processor, switching point, memory, or I/O unit, once such unit has been localized as a source of the error.

Interactive multiprocessor systems refer to systems for the simultaneous processing by a relatively large number of discrete users running jobs with different characteristics. To increase throughput, a reconfigurable system operates by allocating an optimum number of processors, memories, and I/O units to each respective user. In this sense the system "reconfigures" itself by partitioning the system into independently operating units, either on a space-division or time-division multiplex basis.

A *configurable array processor* is a system in which the processors are arranged in an array for processing data that have some geometrical relationship to each other. For example, a two-dimensional array processor may operate on a two-dimensional representation of data to be processed, such as to perform numerical calculations with respect to a set of grid points. If the particular two-dimensional representation is changed to process another job, such as by utilizing a different configuration of grid points, then the system could "reconfigure" itself to another more suitable array configuration.

A *compiler-based system* is a processor configuration that is organized on the basis of the structure of language and operates by direct execution or compilation of instruction sequences in that language. Compilation is the process of translating instructions in a higher level language to instructions that are executed by the system. A reconfigurable system will rearrange its processor configuration to conform with the particular program being compiled, thereby expediting the compilation and execution process.

Microprocessors may be utilized to implement computer systems based on such reconfigurable architectures. The basic system can be implemented by means of a multiprocessor array, together with supervisory and data transfer function controlled by other processors. The arrangement between these processors determines the type of multiprocessor systems implemented. There are several basic types of multiprocessor configurations which may implement a reconfigurable system:

1. Hierarchical
2. Parallel
3. Ring
4. Switched

A hierarchical system (shown in Fig. 9.13) is based on one "master" processor and two or more "slave" processors in a hierarchical relationship. The master processor controls or supervises the operation of the "slave" processors in either a "tightly" or a "loosely" coupled manner.

A parallel system (shown in Fig. 9.14) utilizes two or more processors

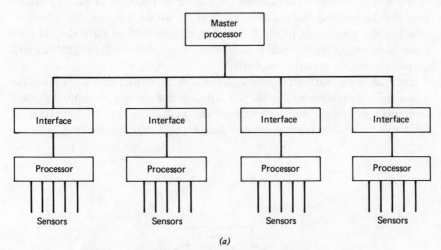

(a)

FIGURE 9.13 HIERARCHICAL MULTIPROCESSOR SYSTEM.

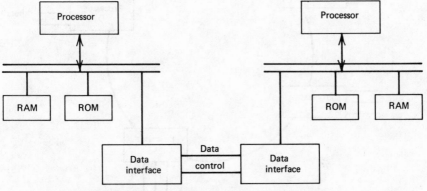

FIGURE 9.14 PARALLEL MULTIPROCESSOR SYSTEM.

that may operate on two or more data streams in parallel. A parallel system may also be configured to operate in parallel on a single data stream as a high reliability processing system.

A ring system (shown in Fig. 9.15) is an array of processors distributed along one or more rings or loops. Data are transferred around the ring and captured by a particular processor according to predetermined criteria.

A switched system (shown in Fig. 9.16) is an array of processors interconnected by a crosspoint switch that directly couples any one processor to any other processor.

In addition to these four general classifications based on structure, a functional classification describing the nature or function of the processors may also be applied. Such a subclassification would describe, for example, whether the processors in the system are all identical or have special purpose functions. This particular subclassification defines homogeneous and nonhomogeneous systems respectively.

Each of these multiprocessor systems can be implemented with microprocessors. Furthermore, with the appropriate hardware and software structures to control and synchronize the multiprocessor configuration, a fully reconfigurable microprocessor architecture may be realized.

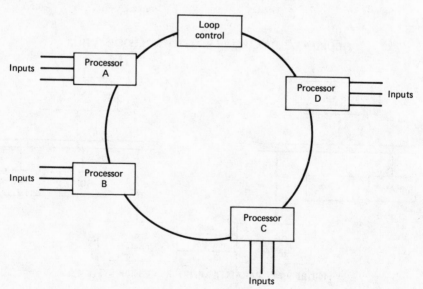

FIGURE 9.15   RING MULTIPROCESSOR SYSTEM.

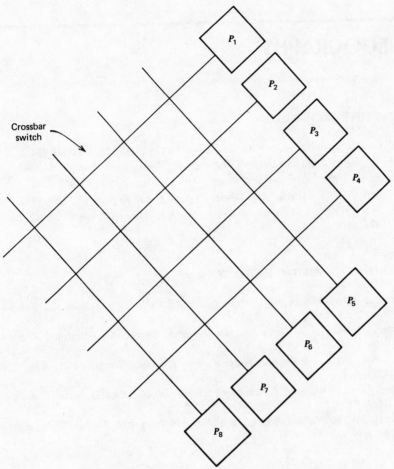

FIGURE 9.16 SWITCHED MULTIPROCESSOR SYSTEM.

BIBLIOGRAPHY

COMPUTER ARCHITECTURE

Bell, C., and Newell, A., *Computer Structures*, McGraw-Hill, New York, 1970.

Chu, Y., *Digital Computer Design Fundamentals*, McGraw-Hill, New York, 1962.

Husson, S. S., *Microprogramming*, Prentice-Hall, Englewood Cliffs, 1970.

Kohonen, T., *Digital Circuits and Devices*, Prentice-Hall, Englewood Cliffs, 1972.

Lorin, H., *Parallelism in Hardware and Software*, Prentice-Hall, Englewood Cliffs, 1972.

MICROPROCESSOR TECHNOLOGY

American Micro-Systems, Inc., *MOS Integrated Circuits*, Van Nostrand Reinhold, New York, 1972.

Camenzind, H. R., *Electronic Integrated System Design*, Van Nostrand Reinhold, New York, 1972.

De Forest, W. S., *Photoresist Materials and Processes*, McGraw-Hill, New York, 1975.

Grove, A. S., *Physics and Technology of Semiconductor Devices*, Wiley, New York, 1967.

Richman, P., *MOS Field Effect Transistors and Integrated Circuits*, Wiley-Interscience, New York, 1973.

MICROPROCESSOR SURVEY

EDN'S First Annual µP Directory, Cahners Publishing Co., Inc., Boston, 1974.

Microprocessor Field Survey and Data Book, AH Systems Inc., Chatsworth, Calif., 1975.

MICROPROCESSOR OPERATION AND PROGRAMMING

4004/4040 Assembly Language Programming Manual, Intel Corporation, Santa Clara, Calif., 1974.

8080 User's Manual, Intel Corporation, Santa Clara, Calif., 1975.

8080 Assembly Language Programming Manual, Intel Corporation, Santa Clara, Calif., 1975.

PL/M High-Level Language Programming Manual, Intel Corporation, Santa Clara, Calif., 1975.

M6800 Microprocessor Applications Manual, Motorola Semiconductor Products Inc., Phoenix, Ariz., 1975.

M6800 Programming Manual, Motorola Semiconductor Products, Inc., Phoenix, Ariz., 1975.

IMP-16C Application Manual, National Semiconductor Corp., Santa Clara, Calif., 1974.

F-8 Microprocessor Applications Notes, Fairchild Semiconductor Components Group, Mountain View, Calif., 1975.

F-8 Microprocessor Programming Guide, Fairchild Semiconductor Components Group, Mountain View, Calif., 1975.

CP1600 Microprocessor Users Manual, General Instrument Corp., Hicksville, NY, 1975.

MICROCOMPUTER SYSTEM DESIGN

Blakeslee, T. R., *Digital Design with Standard MSI and LSI*, Wiley-Interscience. New York, 1975.

Martin, D. P., *Microcomputer Design*, Martin Research Ltd., Chicago, 1974.

MICROPROCESSOR APPLICATIONS

UPC Symbol Specification Manual, Uniform Product Code Council Inc., Alexandria, Va., 1975.

Abramson, N., and Kuo, F. F., Eds., *Computer-Communications Networks*, Prentice-Hall, Englewood Cliffs, 1973.

Fleisher, H. and Maissel, L. I. "Reconfigurable Machine," *IBM Technical Disclosure Bulletin*, IBM Corp., Armonk, NY, March, 1974.

Halsall, F., "A Microprocessor Controlled Interface for Data Transmission," *The Radio and Electronic Engineer*, Vol. 45, No. 3, 131–137 (1975).

ARTICLE COLLECTIONS

Altman, L., Ed., *Microprocessors*, Electronics Magazine Book Series, New York, 1975.

EDN Microprocessor Reprint, Boston, 1975.

Torrero, E. A., Ed., *Microprocessors: New Directions for Designers*, Hayden Book Co., Rochelle Park, NJ, 1975.

PERIODICALS

Computer Design
Digital Design
EDN Magazine
Electronic Design
Electronic Engineering
Electronics
Elektronik
Nikkei Electronics
The Radio and Electronic Engineer
Solid State Technology

GLOSSARY

Access Time: Time between the instant that an address is sent to a memory and the instant that data returns. Since the access time to different locations (addresses) of the memory may be different, the access time specified in a memory device is the path that takes the longest time.

Accumulator: Register and related circuitry that holds one operand for arithmetic and logical operations.

Additional Hardware: Microprocessor chips differ in number of additional ICs required to implement a functioning computer. Generally, timing, I/O control, buffering, and interrupt control require external components.

Address: A number used by the CPU to specify a location in memory.

Addressing Modes: See Memory Addressing Modes.

ALU: Arithmetic-Logic Unit. That part of a CPU which executes adds, subtracts, shifts, AND's, OR's, etc.

Architecture: Organizational structure of a computing system, mainly referring to the CPU or microprocessor.

Assembler: Software that converts an assembly-language program into machine language. The assembler assigns locations in storage to successive instructions and replaces symbolic addresses by machine language equivalents. If the assembler runs on a computer other than that for which it creates the machine language, it is a **Cross-Assembler.**

Assembly Language: An English-like programming language which saves the programmer the trouble of remembering the bit patterns in each instruction; also relieves him of the necessity to keep track of locations of data and instructions in his program.
The assembler operates on a "one-for-one" basis in that each phrase of the language translates directly into a specific machine-language word, as contrasted with **High Level Language.**

Assembly Listing: A printed listing made by the assembler to document an assembly. It shows, line for line, how the assembler interpreted the assembly language program.

Asynchronous Operation: Circuit operation without reliance upon a common timing source. Each circuit operation is terminated (and next operation initiated) by a return signal from the destination denoting completion of an operation. (Contrast with **Synchronous Operation**).

(reprinted with permission of RCA Solid State Division)

Baud: A communications measure of serial data transmission rate; loosely, bits per second but includes character-framing START and STOP bits.

Benchmark Program: A sample program used to evaluate and compare computers. In general, two computers will not use the same number of instructions, memory words, or cycles to solve the same problem.

Bit: An abbreviation of "binary digit". (Single characters in a binary number.)

Bootstrap (Bootstrap Loader): Technique or device for loading first instructions (usually only a few words) of a routine into memory; then using these instructions to bring in the rest of the routine.
The boostrap loader is usually entered manually or by pressing a special console key. See **Load Facility**.

Branch: See **Jump**

Branch Instruction: A decision-making instruction that, on appropriate condition, forces a new address into the program counter. The conditions may be zero result, overflow on add, an external flag raised, etc. One of two alternate program segments in the memory are chosen, depending on the results obtained.

Breakpoint: A location specified by the user at which program execution (real or simulated) is to terminate. Used to aid in locating program errors.

Bus: A group of wires that allow memory, CPU, and I/O devices to exchange words.

Byte: A sequence of n bits operated upon as a unit is called an n-bit byte. The most frequent byte size is 8 bits.

Call Routine: See **Subroutine**

Clock: A device that sends out timing pulses to synchronize the actions of the computer.

Compiler: Software to convert a program in a high-level language such as FORTAN into an assembly language or machine language program.

Cross Assembler: A symbolic language translator that runs on one type of computer to produce machine code for another type of computer. See **Assembler**.

CPU (Central Processing Unit): That part of a computer system that controls the interpretation and execution of instructions. In general, the CPU contains the following elements: Arithmetic-Logic Unit (ALU), Timing and Control, Accumulator, Scratch-pad memory, Program counter and address stack, Instruction register and decode, Parallel data and I/O bus, Memory and I/O control.

Cycle Stealing: A memory cycle stolen from the normal CPU operation for a DMA operation. See **DMA**.

Cycle Time: Time interval at which any set of operations is repeated regularly in the same sequence.

D Register: The accumulator in the COSMAC microprocessor.

Data Pointer: A register holding the memory address of the data (operand) to be used by an instruction. Thus the register "points" to the memory location of the data.

Data Register: Any register which holds data.

Debug: To eliminate programming mistakes, including omissions, from a program.

Debug Programs: Debug programs help the programmer to find errors in his programs while they are running on the computer, and allow him to replace or patch instructions into (or out of) his program.

Designator: The three 4-bit registers P, X, and N in the COSMAC microprocessor are called designators. P and X are used to designate which one of the sixteen 16-bit scratch-pad registers is used as the current program counter and the data pointer, respectively.
N can designate: one of the scratch-pad registers; an I/O device or command: a new value in P or X; and a further definition of an instruction.

Diagnostic programs: These programs check the various hardware parts of a system for proper operation; CPU diagnostics check the CPU, memory diagnostics check the memory, and so forth.

Direct Addressing: The address of an instruction or operand is completely specified in an instruction without reference to a base register or index register.

DMA: Direct Memory Access. A mechanism that allows an input/output device to take control of the CPU for one or more memory cycles, in order to write to or read from memory. The order of executing the program steps (instructions) remains unchanged.

Editor: As an aid in preparing source programs, certain programs have been developed that manipulate text material. These programs, called editors, text editors, or paper tape editors make it possible to compose assembly language programs on-line, or on a stand-alone system.

Execute: The process of interpreting an instruction and performing the indicated operations (s).

Fetch: A process of addressing the memory and reading into the CPU the information word, or byte, stored at the addressed location. Most often, fetch refers to the reading out of an instruction from the memory.

Firmware: Software that is implemented in ROM's.

Fixed-instruction Computer (Stored-Instruction Computer): The instruction set of a computer is fixed by the manufacturer. The users will design application programs using this instruction set (in contrast to the **Microprogrammable Computer** for which the users must design their own instruction set and thus customize the computer for their needs.)

Fixed Memory: See ROM

Flag Lines: Inputs to a microprocessor controlled by I/O devices and tested by branch instructions.

Fortran: A high-leevl programming language generally for scientific use, expressed in algebraic notation. Short for "Formula Translator".

Guard: A mechanism to terminate program execution (real or simulated) upon access to data at a specified memory location. Used in debugging.

Hardware: Physical equipment forming a computer system.

Hexadecimal: Number system using 0, 1, ... , A, B, C, D, E, F to represent all the possible values of a 4-bit digit. The decimal equivalent is 0 to 15. Two hexadecimal digits can be used to specify a byte.

High-Level Language: Programming language that generates machine codes from problem- or function-oriented statements. FORTRAN, COBOL, and BASIC are three commonly used high-level languages. A single functional statement may translate into a series of instructions or subroutines in machine language, in contrast to a low-level (assembly) language in which statements translate on a one-for-one basis.

Immediate Addressing: The method of addressing an instruction in which the operand is located in the instruction itself or in the memory location immediately following the instruction.

Immediate Data: Data that immediately follows an instruction in memory, and is used as an operand by that instruction.

Indexed Addressing: An addressing mode, in which the address part of an instruction is modified by the contents in an auxiliary (index) register during the execution of that instruction.

Index Register: A register that contains a quantity which may be used to modify memory address.

Indirect Addressing: A means of addressing which the address of the operand is specified by an auxiliary register or memory location specified by the instruction rather than by bits in the instruction itself.

Input-Output (I/O): General term for the equipment used to communicate with a computer CPU; or the data involved in that communcation.

Instruction: A set of bits that defines a computer operation, and is a basic command understood by the CPU. It may move data, do arithmetic and logic functions, control I/O devices, or make decisions as to which instruction to execute next.

Instruction Cycle: The process of fetching an instruction from memory and executing it.

Instruction Length: The number of words needed to store an instruction. It is one word in most computers, but some will use multiple words to form one instruction. Multiple-word instructions have different instruction execution times depending on the length of the instruction.

Instruction Repertoire: See Instruction Set

Instruction Set: The set of general-purpose instructions available with a given computer. In general, different machines have different instruction sets.
The number of instructions only partially indicates the quality of an instruction set. Some instructions may only be slightly different from one another; others rarely may be used. Instruction sets should be compared

using benchmark programs typical of the application, to determine execution times, and memory requirements.

Instruction Time: The time required to fetch an instruction from memory and then execute it.

Interpreter: A program that fetches and executes "instructions" **(pseudo instructions)** written in a higher level language. The higher-level language program is a **pseudo program.** Contrast with **Compiler.**

Interrupt Request: A signal to the computer that temporarily suspends the normal sequence of a routine and transfers control to a special routine. Operation can be resumed from this point later. Ability to handle interrupts is very useful in communication applications where it allows the microprocessor to service many channels.

Interrupt Mask (Interrupt Enable): A mechanism that allows the program to specify whether or not interrupt requests will be accepted.

Interrupt Service Routine: A routine (program) to properly store away to the stack the present status of the machine in order to respond to an interrupt request; perform the "real work" required by the interrupt; restore the saved status of the machine; and then resume the operation of the interrupted program.

I/O Control Electronics (I/O Controller): The control electronics required to interface an I/O device to a computer CPU.
The powerfulness and usefulness of a CPU is very closely associated with the range of I/O devices that can be connected to it. One can not usually simply plug them into the CPU. The I/O Control Electronics will do the "matchmaking". The complexity and cost of the Control Electronics are very much determined by both the hardware and software I/O architecture of the CPU.

I/O Interface: See I/O Control Electronics

I/O Port: A connection to a CPU that is configured (or programmed) to provide a data path between the CPU and the external devices, such as keyboard, display, reader, etc. An I/O port of a microprocessor may be an input or an output port, or it may be bidirectional.

Jump: A departure from the normal one-step incrementing of the program counter. By forcing a new value (address) into the program counter the next instruction can be fetched from an arbitray location (either further ahead or back).
For example, a program jump can be used to go from the main program to a subroutine, from a subroutine back to the main program, or from the end of a short routine back to the beginning of the same routine to form a loop. See also the Branch Instruction. If you reached this point from Branch, you have executed a Jump. Now Return.

Linkage: See Subroutine

Load Facility: A hardware facility to allow program loading using DMA. It makes bootstrap unnecessary.

Loader: A program to read a program from an input device into RAM. May be part of a package of utility programs.

Loop: A self-contained series of instructions in which the last instruction can cause repetition of the series until a terminal condition is reached. Branch instructions are used to test the conditions in the loop to determine if the loop should be continued or terminated.

Low-Level Language: See **Assembly Language**

Machine: A term for a computer (of historical origin).

Machine Code: See Machine Language

Machine Cycle: The basic CPU cycle. In one machine cycle an address may be sent to memory and one word (data or instruction) read or written, or, in one machine cycle a fetched instruction can be executed.

Machine Language: The numeric form of specifying instructions, ready for loading into memory and execution by the machine. This is the lowest-level language in which to write programs. The value of every bit in every instruction in the program must be specified (e.g., by giving a string of binary, octal, or hexadecimal digits for the contents of each word in memory).

Machine State: See **State Code**

Macro (Macroinstruction): A symbolic source language statement that is expanded by the assembler into one or more machine language instructions, relieving the programmer of having to write out frequently occurring instruction sequences.

Manufacturer's Support: It includes application information, software assistance, components for prototyping, availability of hardware in all configurations from chips to systems, and fast response to requests for engineering assistance.

Memory: That part of a computer that holds data and instructions. Each instructions or datum is assigned a unique address that is used by the CPU when fetching or storing the information.

Memory Address Register: The CPU register that holds the address of the memory location being accessed.

Memory Addressing Modes: The method of specifying the memory location of an operand. Common addressing modes are—direct, immediate, relative, indexed, and indirect. These modes are important factors in program efficiency.

Microcomputer: A computer whose CPU is a microprocessor. A microcomputer is an entire system with microprocessor, memory, and input-output controllers.

Microprocessor: Frequently called "a computer on a chip". The microprocessor is, in reality, a set of one, or a few, LSI circuits capable of performing the essential functions of a computer CPU.

Microprogrammable Computer: A computer in which the internal CPU control signal sequence for performing instructions are generated from a ROM. By changing the ROM contents, the instruction set can be changed. This contrasts with a Fixed-Instruction Computer in which the instruction set can not be readily changed.

Mnemonics: Symbolic names or abbreviations for instructions, registers, memory locations, etc. A technique for improving the efficiency of the human memory.

Multiple Processing: Configuring two or more processors in a single system, operating out of a common memory. This arrangement permits execution of as many programs as there are processors.

Nesting: Subroutines that are called by subroutines are said to be nested. The nesting level is the number of times nesting can be repeated.

Nibble: A sequence of 4 bits operated upon as a unit. Also see Byte.

Object Program: Program that is the output of an automatic coding system, such as the assembler. Often the object program is a machine-language program ready for execution.

On-Line System: A system of I/O devices in which the operation of such devices is under the control of the CPU, and in which information reflecting current activity is introduced into the data processing or controlling system as soon as it occurs.

Op Code (Operation Code): A code that represents specific operations of an instruction.

Operating System: System software controlling the overall operation of a multipurpose computer system, including such tasks as memory allocation, input and output distribution, interrupt processing, and job scheduling.

Page: A natural grouping of memory locations by higher-order address bits. In an 8-bit microprocessor, $2^8 = 256$ consecutive bytes often may constitute a page. Then words on the same page only differ in the lower-order 8 address bits.

PLA (Programmable Logic Array): A PLA is an array of logic elements that can be programmed to perform a specific logic function. In this sense, the array of logic elements can be as simple as a gate or as complex as a ROM. The array can be programmed (normally mask programmable) so that a given input combination produces a known output function.

Pointer: Registers in the CPU that contain memory addresses. See Program Counter and Data Pointer.

Program: A collection of instructions properly ordered to perform some particular task.

Program Counter: A CPU register that specifies the address of the next instruction to be fetched and executed. Normally it is incremented automatically each time an instruction is fetched.

PROM (Programmable Read-Only Memory): An integrated-circuit memory array that is manufactured with a pattern of either all logical zeros or ones and has a specific pattern written into it by the user by a special hardware programmer. Some PROMs, called EAROMs, Electrically Alterable Read-Only Memory, can be erased and reprogrammed.

Prototyping Kit: A hardware system used to breadboard a microprocessor-based product. Contains CPU, memory, basic I/O, power supply, switches and lamps, provisions for custom I/O controllers, memory expansion, and often, a utility program in fixed memory (ROM).

Pseudo Instruction: See **Interpreter**

Pseudo Program: See **Interpreter**

RAM (Random Access Memory): Any type of memory that has both read and write capability. It is randomly accessible in the sense that the time required to read from or to write into the memory, is independent of the location of the memory where data was most recently read from or written into. In contrast, in a **Serial Access Memory**, this time is variable.

Register: A fast-access circuit used to store bits or words in a CPU. Registers play a key role in CPU operations. In most applications, the efficiency of programs is related to the number of registers.

Relative Addressing: The address of the data referred to is the address given in the instruction plus some other number. The "other number" can be the address of the instruction, the address of the first location of the current memory page, or a number stored in a register. Relative addressing permits the machine to relocate a program or a block of data by changing only one number.

Return Routine: See **Subroutine**

ROM: Read-Only Memory (Fixed Memory) is any type of memory that cannot be readily rewritten; ROM requires a masking operation during production to permanently record program or data patterns in it. The information is stored on a permanent basis and used repetitively. Such storage is useful for programs or tables of data that remain fixed and is usually randomly accessible.

Routine: Usaully refers to a sub-program, i.e., the task performed by the routine is less complex. A program may include routines. See **Program**.

Scratch-Pad Memory: RAM or registers that are used to store temporary intermediate results (data), or memory addressed (pointers).

Serial Memory (Serial Access Memory): Any type of memory in which the time required to read from or write into the memory is dependent on the location in the memory. This type of meory has to wait while nondesired memory locations are accessed. Examples are paper tape, disc, magnetic tape, CCD, etc. In a Random Access Memory, access time is constant.

Simulators: Software simulators are sometimes used in the debug process to simulate the execution of machine-language programs using another computer (often a timesharing system). These simulators are especially useful if the actual computer is not available. They may facilitate the debugging by providing access to internal registers of the CPU which are not brought out to external pins in the hardware.

Snapshots: Capture of the entire state of a machine (real or simulated)— memory contents, registers, flags, etc.

Software: Computer programs. Often used to denote general-purpose programs provided by the manufacturer, such as assembler, editor, compiler, etc.

Source Program: Computer program written in a language designed for ease of expression of a class of problems or procedures, by humans: symbolic or algebraic.

Stack: A sequence of registers and/or memory locations used in LIFO fashion (last-in-first-out). **A stack pointer** specifies the last-in entry (or where the next-in entry will go).

Stack Pointer: The counter, or register, used to address a stack in the memory. See Stack.

Stand-Alone System: A microcomputer software development system that runs on a microcomputer without connection to another computer or a time-sharing system. This system includes an assembler, editor, and debugging aids. It may include some of the features of a prototyping kit.

State Code: A coded indication of what state the CPU is—responding to an interrupt, servicing a DMA request, executing an I/O instruction, etc.

Subroutine: A subprogram (group of instructions) reached from more than one place in a **main program**. The process of passing control from the main program to a subroutine is a **subroutine call**, and the mechanism is a **subroutine linkage**. Often data or data addresses are made available by the main program to the subroutine. The process of returning control from subroutine to main program is **subroutine return**. The linkage automatically returns control to the original position in the main program or to another subroutine. See Nesting.

Subroutine Linkage: See **Subroutine**

Support: See **Manufacturer's Support**

Synchronous Operation: Use of a common timing source (clock) to time circuit or data transfer operations. (Contrast with **Asynchronous** operation)

Syntax: Formal structure. The rules governing sentence structure in a language such as assembly language or Fortran.

Terminal: An Input-Output device at which data leaves or enters a computer system, e.g., teletype terminal, CRT terminal, etc.

Test and Branch: See **Branch Instruction.**

Unbundling: Pricing certain types of software and services separately from the hardware.

Utility Program: A program providing basic conveniences, such as capability for loading and saving programs, for observing and changing values in a computer, and for initiating program execution. The utility program eliminates the need for "re-inventing the wheel" every time a designer wants to perform a common function.

Word: The basic group of bits that is manipulated (read in, stored, added, read out, etc.) by the computer in a single step. Two types of words are used in every computer: Data Words and Instruction Words. Data words contain the information to be manipulated. Instruction words cause the computer to execute a particular operation.

Word Length: The number of bits in the computer word. The longer the word length, the greater the precision (number of significant digits). In general, the longer the word length, the richer the instruction set, and the more varied the addressing modes.

APPENDIX

MICROPROCESSOR MANUFACTURERS DIRECTORY

Advanced Micro Devices Inc.
901 Thompson Place
Sunnyvale, Calif., 94086
(408) 732-2400

American Micro-Systems, Inc.
3800 Homestead Road
Santa Clara, Calif., 95051
(408) 246-0330

Electronic Arrays, Inc.
550 Middlefield Road
Mountain View, Calif., 94043
(415) 964-4321

Fairchild Semiconductor Components
   Group
464 Ellis Street
Mountain View, Calif., 94042
(415) 962-5011

Fujitsu Ltd.
Marunouchi
Tokyo, Japan

General Instrument Corporation
Microelectronics Division
600 W. John Street
Hicksville, NY, 11802
(516) 733-3107

Hitachi Ltd.
Otemachi
Chiyoda-ku
Tokyo, Japan

Intel Corporation
3065 Bowers Avenue
Santa Clara, Calif., 95051
(408) 246-7501

Intersil, Inc.
10900 Tantau Avenue
Cupertino, Calif., 95014
(408) 257-5450

MOS Technology, Inc.
950 Rittenhouse Road
Norristown, Pa, 19401
(215) 666-7950

Monolithic Memories, Inc.
1165 E. Arques Avenue
Sunnyvale, Calif., 94086
(408) 739-3535

Mostek
1215 W. Crosby Road
Carrollton, Tx, 75006
(214) 242-0444

Motorola Semiconductor
Box 20912
Phoenix, Az, 85036
(602) 244-3965

National Semiconductor Corporation
2900 Semiconductor Drive
Santa Clara, Calif., 95051
(408) 732-5000

Raytheon Company
Semiconductor Division
350 Ellis Street
Mountain View, Calif., 94042
(415) 968-9211

RCA Corporation
Solid State Division
Sommerville, NJ, 08776
(201) 685-6000

Rockwell International Corporation
Microelectronic Device Division
3310 Miraloma Avenue
Anaheim, Calif., 92803
(714) 632-3729

Scientific Microsystems, Inc.
520 Clyde Avenue
Mountain View, Calif., 94043
(415) 964-5700

Signetics Corporation
811 E. Arques Avenue
Sunnyvale, Calif., 94186
(408) 739-7700

Texas Instruments Inc.
P.O. Box 5012
Dallas, Tx, 75222
(214) 238-2011

Toshiba America Inc.
280 Park Avenue
New York, NY,
(212) 557-0200

Transitron Electronic Corporation
168 Albion Street
Wakefield, Ma, 01880
(617) 245-4500

Western Digital Corporation
19242 Red Hill Avenue
Newport Beach, Calif., 92663
(714) 557-3550

INDEX